KENNETH & GLORIA COPELAND

PROTECTION
PROMISES

Harrison House
Tulsa, Oklahoma

Protection Promises
ISBN 1-57794-201-9   30-0708
Copyright © 1999 Kenneth and Gloria Copeland
Kenneth Copeland Ministries
Fort Worth, Texas 76192-0001

Published by Harrison House, Inc.
P.O. Box 35035
Tulsa, Oklahoma 74153

TABLE of CONTENTS

Preface 5

Chapter 1   Never Alone 9
            When You Feel Alone 11
            When You Have No Resources 16
            When Trouble Surrounds You 22
            When You Need God's Strength 24

Chapter 2   God's Contract of Protection .. 29
            His Commitment to Your Safety ... 31
            His Commitment to Your
               Long Life 36
            His Commitment to Act in
               Love and Mercy 41
            His Commitment to Respond
               to His Name 45

Chapter 3   Secure in Jesus 49
            Resting in His Victory 51
            Pleading the Blood 56
            Acting Confidently 59

Chapter 4   The Right Place to Be 63

Chapter 5   Guided Safely by God's Word .. 75
            Preserved by His Word 78
            Directed in Safe Paths 83
            Kept in a Protected Place 93
            Equipped to Hear God's Voice 101
            Given Words of Power 103
            Caused to Sleep in Peace 106

Chapter 6   Hidden in God 111
             Your Only Salvation 113
             Your Hiding Place 117
             Your Place of Refuge 122
             Your Way of Escape 130

Chapter 7   Freedom From Fear 133
             Overcoming Terror 136
             Overcoming the Spirit of Fear 140
             Overcoming Fear
               of Abandonment 144
             Overcoming Fear of Man 147
             Overcoming Evil Reports 156
             Angels—Agents of Protection 160

Chapter 8   Safety for Your Family 167

Chapter 9   A Spectator in the Battle 179
             The Battle Is the Lord's 182
             God Delivers His People 183
             An Enemy to Your Enemies 188
             Your Strength and Shield 194
             Spectator in the Battle 200

Chapter 10 Enforcing Jesus' Victory 207
             Enforce His Victory 209
             Act in His Name 221
             Enjoy His Peace 226

Word/Scripture Index 237

P R E F A C E

It would be wonderful if this were a trouble-free world. But it isn't. Our world is filled with harm, terror and acts of darkness as close as our own neighborhoods.

But as dark as this world may be, the future is secure for those who know how to stand unmoved and unafraid on the promises of God's Word. Tomorrow is bright for those who know how to stay in faith until even the most threatening situations line up with His promises of safety and well-being.

Protection Promises is a collection of scriptures straight from the heart of God to you. Every day Gloria and I believe God, and we plead the blood of Jesus over our family, our staff and our Partners. We believe for their protection and their deliverance.

We pray filled with boldness and faith because we know the promises God has made to His people. We know that when Jesus was delivered from death by the power of the Holy Spirit, He did not come out empty-handed. He came triumphant over Satan, death and the grave, saying, "*All power has been given unto Me...therefore, go ye...and lo, I will be with you always.*"

Satan tries to come against God's people through threats, terror and the actions of those he has deceived. This is no surprise to God. Psalm 23 tells us that not only did God know this would happen, but He also made provision for our safety in the midst of it. With the promises of God's Word and the direction of Jesus, our Great Shepherd, we can have victory over every activity of the enemy in this life on earth.

I will never forget the night when I received the most unusual revelation of our position of safety in the victory Jesus had won. Gloria and I had gone to a church where a friend of ours was singing. We sat a few rows back in the middle section. Gloria was on one side of me and a fellow minister was on the other.

As our friend sang a particular song about the heavenly feast of God, he spoke of the banquet table that is being prepared and set for us right now. Then he mentioned Psalm 23. My mind went over the Psalm as I listened... "*The Lord is my shepherd; I shall not want.... Thou preparest a table before me in the presence of mine enemies....*"

Then, all of a sudden, I heard the Spirit of God louder than the words of the song. He said, *That is not a heavenly feast in the 23rd Psalm.*

My body literally jumped while I was sitting there. Gloria noticed and so did the minister sitting beside me. But I didn't say a word right then. I waited until after the service; then I ran outside because I was so full of revelation of the Word of God. Even our friend who was ministering and singing on the platform saw me jump during the song, and he followed me.

Once we were all out of the building, I told them what God had shown me about Psalm 23. He said, *The table in Psalm 23 is not a heavenly table. It's an earthly table. I prepare a table before you in the presence of your enemies. You don't have enemies in heaven. I want My family to come to the table I have prepared before their enemies while they are on earth. They don't have to put it off until they get to heaven.*

And the Lord said, *The only thing I'm having trouble with is getting My kids to come to the table. They all want to go to heaven first.*

We had church again right there!

Your Heavenly Father has prepared a banquet for you before your enemies. When you have God protecting you, your enemies are His enemies (Exodus 23:22-23). Your enemies may be on earth, but so is the Psalm 23 table God has prepared for you. God has given you His promises of protection in His Word and His covenant of protection through salvation in Jesus. *Salvation* is defined in *Vine's Expository Dictionary of Biblical Words* as "material and temporal deliverance from danger and apprehension, preservation, pardon, restoration, healing, wholeness and soundness." No wonder there is a banquet table set! He's ready for you to celebrate now on earth.

As you study the Bible every day, meditate God's promises of protection and deposit them into your heart. Speak out loud His promises of protection over your life. God promises to care for you and protect you in so many ways. He wants you to know the victory has been won. The enemy has been defeated. Jesus has conquered Satan. He has fought every battle and won the victory for you. You don't have to wait to get to heaven. Your protection in the here and now is assured by the blood of Jesus.

From now on, don't be moved by threatening circumstances or situations. Study these *Protection Promises* and let God's Word build a shield of protection around you.

Treat these promises and scriptural foundations of His protection like you treated His promise of salvation—believe them, act on them, receive them and speak them out in faith. If you do, you'll sleep through the worst of storms, and when you arise in the peace of God and the authority of His Word, you'll be the devil's worst nightmare!

Kenneth and Gloria Copeland

Chapter 1

Never Alone

In my distress I called upon the Lord, and cried unto my God: he heard my voice out of his temple, and my cry came before him, even into his ears.... He delivered me from my strong enemy, and from them which hated me: for they were too strong for me.... He brought me forth also into a large place; he delivered me, because he delighted in me.

Psalm 18:6, 17, 19

Thus saith the Lord of hosts...
he that toucheth you toucheth
the apple of his eye.
Zechariah 2:8

You are not the part-time focus of God's attention. You are His delight and the full-time object of His affection. Israel's King David wrote, "*Keep me as the apple of the eye, hide me under the shadow of thy wings*" (Psalm 17:8). That's the heart of your Heavenly Father.

His promises to Abraham and Moses show that man's well-being is God's number one concern. He sent His own Son, Jesus, to take every curse of the Law on His own body for us, so that we could walk in all the benefits of God's protection, wholeness and prosperity. From beginning to end, He tells you in His Word how much He loves you by demonstrating how protective He is of His people.

God is not someone who is hard to get hold of when you get in trouble. He is not someone who can't hear you call out his name when you have a need. In fact, He is waiting for those who will take His promises seriously. For the sake of His Word and His Name, He will rush to the aid of those who call on Him. He wants to be involved in securing our lives not only in heaven, but also while we live down here.

So don't ever accept the lie that you are alone and forgotten. The Lord knows right where you are.

Trust Him, turn to Him, give Him an opportunity to prove His love for you in time of trouble—He'll shake heaven and hell to deliver you and bring you to a place of safety.

When You Feel Alone

Psalm 3:4-5

NIV—To the Lord I cry aloud, and he answers me from his holy hill. Selah. I lie down and sleep; I wake again, because the Lord sustains me.

AMP—With my voice I cry to the Lord, and He hears and answers me out of His holy hill. Selah [pause, and calmly think of that]! I lay down and slept; I wakened again, for the Lord sustains me.

Moffatt—When I call out to the Eternal, he answers me from his sacred hill. I laid me down to sleep, and this morning I waken, for the Eternal upholds me.

KJV—I cried unto the Lord with my voice, and he heard me out of his holy hill. Selah. I laid me down and slept; I awaked; for the Lord sustained me.

Psalm 18:3

KJV—I will call upon the Lord, who is worthy to be praised: so shall I be saved from mine enemies.

AMP—I will call upon the Lord, Who is to be praised; so shall I be saved from my enemies.

Moffatt—The Eternal is to be praised!—I call to him, and I am rescued from my foes.

NIV—I call to the Lord, who is worthy of praise, and I am saved from my enemies.

Psalm 18:4-19

KJV—The sorrows of death compassed me, and the floods of ungodly men made me afraid. The sorrows of hell compassed me about: the snares of death prevented me. In my distress I called upon the Lord, and cried unto my God: he heard my voice out of his temple, and my cry came before him, even into his ears.

Then the earth shook and trembled; the foundations also of the hills moved and were shaken, because he was wroth. There went up a smoke out of his nostrils, and fire out of his mouth devoured: coals were kindled by it. He bowed the heavens also, and came down: and darkness was under his feet. And he rode upon a cherub, and did fly: yea, he did fly upon the wings of the wind. He made darkness his secret place;

his pavilion round about him were dark waters and thick clouds of the skies. At the brightness that was before him his thick clouds passed, hail stones and coals of fire. The Lord also thundered in the heavens, and the Highest gave his voice; hail stones and coals of fire. Yea, he sent out his arrows, and scattered them; and he shot out lightnings, and discomfited them. Then the channels of waters were seen, and the foundations of the world were discovered at thy rebuke, O Lord, at the blast of the breath of thy nostrils.

He sent from above, he took me, he drew me out of many waters. He delivered me from my strong enemy, and from them which hated me: for they were too strong for me. They prevented me in the day of my calamity: but the Lord was my stay. He brought me forth also into a large place; he delivered me, because he delighted in me.

Psalm 31:1-2

KJV—O Lord...Bow down thine ear to me; deliver me speedily.

AMP—O Lord...Bow down Your ear to me, deliver me speedily!

Moffatt—O thou Eternal...Turn thine ear to me, delay not to deliver me.

NIV—O Lord...Turn your ear to me, come quickly to my rescue.

Psalm 55:16-17

KJV—I will call upon God; and the Lord shall save me. Evening, and morning, and at noon, will I pray, and cry aloud: and he shall hear my voice.

AMP—I will call upon God; and the Lord will save me. Evening and morning and at noon will I utter my complaint and moan and sigh, and He will hear my voice.

Moffatt—I call to God, and the Eternal helps me; evening, morning, and at noon, I moan and wail. He will hear my cry.

NIV—I call to God, and the Lord saves me. Evening, morning and noon I cry out in distress, and he hears my voice.

Psalm 108:5-6

KJV—Be thou exalted, O God, above the heavens: and thy glory above all the earth; That thy beloved may be delivered: save with thy right hand, and answer me.

AMP—Be exalted, O God, above the heavens, and Your glory be over all the earth; That Your beloved [followers] may be delivered, save with Your right hand, and answer us! [or me]!

Moffatt—Up, O God, high over heaven! Up with thy glory over all the earth! To the rescue of thy dear folk! Save by thy right hand, answer our entreaty.

NIV—Be exalted, O God, above the heavens, and let your glory be over all the earth. Save us and help us with your right hand, that those you love may be delivered.

Psalm 145:18-20

KJV—The Lord is nigh unto all them that call upon him, to all that call upon him in truth. He will fulfil the desire of them that fear him: he also will hear their cry, and will save them. The Lord preserveth all them that love him.

AMP—The Lord is near to all who call upon Him, to all who call upon Him sincerely and in truth. He will fulfill the desire of those who reverently and worshipfully fear Him, He also will hear their cry, and will save them. The Lord preserves all those who love Him.

Moffatt—The Eternal is near all who call on him, who call on him sincerely; he satisfies his worshippers, he hears their cry and helps them; the Eternal preserves all who love him.

NIV—The Lord is near to all who call on him, to all who call on him in truth. He fulfills the desires of those who fear him; he hears their cry and saves them. The Lord watches over all who love him.

Isaiah 59:1

KJV—The Lord's hand is not shortened, that it cannot save; neither his ear heavy, that it cannot hear.

AMP—The Lord's hand is not shortened, that it cannot save; nor His ear dull with deafness that it cannot hear.

Moffatt—The Eternal's hand is not too short to save, the Eternal's ear is not too dull to hear!

NIV—The arm of the Lord is not too short to save, nor his ear too dull to hear.

When You Have No Resources

2 Chronicles 14:11

KJV—Lord, it is nothing with thee to help, whether with many, or with them that have no power.

AMP—O Lord, there is none besides You to help, and no difference to You whether him You help is mighty or powerless.

Moffatt—O Eternal, thou art the only one to help the weak against the mighty.

NIV—Lord, there is no one like you to help the powerless against the mighty.

Psalm 8:2

KJV—Out of the mouth of babes and sucklings hast thou ordained strength because of thine enemies, that thou mightest still the enemy and the avenger.

AMP—Out of the mouth of babes and unweaned infants You have established strength because of Your foes, that You might silence the enemy and the avenger.

NIV—From the lips of children and infants you have ordained praise because of your enemies, to silence the foe and the avenger.

TLB—You have taught the little children to praise you perfectly. May their example shame and silence your enemies!

Psalm 12:5

KJV—For the oppression of the poor, for the sighing of the needy, now will I arise, saith the Lord; I will set him in safety from him that puffeth at him.

AMP—Now will I arise, says the Lord, because the poor are oppressed, because of groans of the needy; I will set him in safety and in the salvation for which he pants.

Moffatt—"The weak are being crushed, the needy sigh; So I take action," says the Eternal One, "and set them safe where they long to be."

NIV—"Because of the oppression of the weak and the groaning of the needy, I will now arise," says the Lord. "I will protect them from those who malign them."

Psalm 34:6

KJV—This poor man cried, and the Lord heard him, and saved him out of all his troubles.

AMP—This poor man cried, and the Lord heard him, and saved him out of all his troubles.

Moffatt—Here is a poor man whose cry the Eternal heard, and helped him out of all his troubles.

NIV—This poor man called, and the Lord heard him; he saved him out of all his troubles.

Psalm 35:10

KJV—All my bones shall say, Lord, who is like unto thee, which deliverest the poor from him that is too strong for him, yea, the poor and the needy from him that spoileth him?

AMP—All my bones shall say, Lord, who is like You, You Who deliver the poor and the afflicted from him who is too strong for him, yes, the poor and the needy from him who snatches away his goods?

Moffatt—All my being shall exclaim, "O thou Eternal, who is like thee, O rescuer of the weak from stronger powers, O rescuer of the wretched from destroyers!"

NIV—My whole being will exclaim, "Who is like you, O Lord? You rescue the poor from those too strong for them, the poor and needy from those who rob them."

Psalm 40:17

KJV—I am poor and needy; yet the Lord thinketh upon me: thou art my help and my deliverer.

AMP—I am poor and needy, yet the Lord takes thought and plans for me. You are my help and my deliverer.

Moffatt—I am weak and wretched; yet the Eternal will take thought for me. Thou art my help and my deliverer.

NIV—I am poor and needy; may the Lord think of me. You are my help and my deliverer.

Psalm 41:1-2

KJV—Blessed is he that considereth the poor: the Lord will deliver him in time of trouble. The Lord will preserve him, and keep him alive; and he shall be blessed upon the earth: and thou wilt not deliver him unto the will of his enemies.

AMP—Blessed—happy, fortunate [to be envied]—is he who considers the weak and the poor; the Lord will deliver him in the time of evil and trouble. The Lord will protect him, and keep him alive; he shall be called blessed in the land; and You will not deliver him to the will of his enemies.

Moffatt—Happy is he who remembers the weak and the poor! The Eternal will deliver him on the day of trouble; the Eternal will

Never
Alone

preserve his life, nor hand him over to his eager foes.

NIV—Blessed is he who has regard for the weak; the Lord delivers him in times of trouble. The Lord will protect him and preserve his life; he will bless him in the land and not surrender him to the desire of his foes.

Psalm 109:30-31

KJV—I will greatly praise the Lord with my mouth.... For he shall stand at the right hand of the poor, to save him from those that condemn his soul.

AMP—I will give great praise and thanks to the Lord with my mouth.... For He will stand at the right hand of the poor and needy, to save him from those who condemn his life.

Moffatt—I will give thanks aloud to the Eternal...for he supports a helpless man, to save him from his persecutors.

NIV—With my mouth I will greatly extol the Lord.... For he stands at the right hand of the needy one, to save his life from those who condemn him.

Isaiah 25:4

KJV—For thou hast been a strength to the poor, a strength to the needy in his distress, a refuge from the storm, a shadow from the heat, when the blast of the terrible ones is as a storm against the wall.

AMP—For You have been a stronghold to the poor, a stronghold to the needy in his distress, a shelter from the storm, a shade from the heat; for the blast of the ruthless ones is like a rainstorm against a wall.

NIV—You have been a refuge for the poor, a refuge for the needy in his distress, a shelter from the storm and a shade from the heat. For the breath of the ruthless is like a storm driving against a wall.

NAS—For Thou hast been a defense for the helpless, A defense for the needy in his distress, A refuge from the storm, a shade from the heat; For the breath of the ruthless is like a rain storm against a wall.

Isaiah 40:28-29

KJV—The Lord...giveth power to the faint; and to them that have no might he increaseth strength.

AMP—The Lord...gives power to the faint and weary, and to him who has no might He increases strength—causing it to multiply and making it abound.

Moffatt—The Eternal...never faints, never is weary, his insight is unsearchable; into the weary he puts power, and adds new strength to the weak.

NIV—The Lord...gives strength to the weary and increases the power of the weak.

Daniel 10:18-19

KJV—There came again and touched me one like the appearance of a man, and he strengthened me, And said, O man greatly beloved, fear not: peace be unto thee, be strong, yea, be strong. And when he had spoken unto me, I was strengthened.

AMP—There touched me again one whose appearance was like that of a man, and he strengthened me. And he said, O man greatly beloved, fear not; peace be to you, be strong, yes, be strong. And when he had spoken to me, I was strengthened.

Moffatt—One in the likeness of a man again touched me and strengthened me, saying, "O man greatly loved by God, fear not; all good be yours; be strong, be brave." At his words I gained strength.

NIV—Again the one who looked like a man touched me and gave me strength. "Do not be afraid, O man highly esteemed," he said. "Peace! Be strong now; be strong." When he spoke to me, I was strengthened.

When Trouble Surrounds You

Psalm 37:39

KJV—The salvation of the righteous is of the Lord: he is their strength in the time of trouble.

AMP—The salvation of the [consistently] righteous is of the Lord; He is their refuge and secure stronghold in the time of trouble.

NIV—The salvation of the righteous comes from the Lord; he is their stronghold in time of trouble.

TLB—The Lord saves the godly! He is their salvation and their refuge when trouble comes.

Psalm 50:15

KJV—Call upon me in the day of trouble: I will deliver thee, and thou shalt glorify me.

AMP—Call on Me in the day of trouble; I will deliver you, and you shall honor and glorify Me.

Moffatt—Call to me in your hour of need, then I will rescue you, and you shall honour me.

NIV—Call upon me in the day of trouble; I will deliver you, and you will honor me.

Psalm 91:15

KJV—He shall call upon me, and I will answer him: I will be with him in trouble; I will deliver him, and honour him.

AMP—He shall call upon Me, and I will answer him; I will be with him in trouble, I will deliver him and honor him.

NIV—He will call upon me, and I will answer him; I will be with him in trouble, I will deliver him and honor him.

TLB—When he calls on me I will answer; I will be with him in trouble, and rescue him and honor him.

Psalm 107:6-7

KJV—They cried unto the Lord in their trouble, and he delivered them out of their distresses. And he led them forth by the right way, that they might go to a city of habitation.

AMP—They cried to the Lord in their trouble, and He delivered them out of their distresses. He led them forth by the straight and right way, that they might go to a city where they might establish their homes.

Moffatt—They cried to the Eternal in their need, to save them from their evil plight, and straight he led them to a settled town.

NIV—They cried out to the Lord in their trouble, and he delivered them from their distress. He led them by a straight way to a city where they could settle.

When You Need God's Strength

Job 36:5

KJV—Behold, God is mighty, and despiseth not any: he is mighty in strength and wisdom.

NKJV—Behold, God is mighty, but despises no one; He is mighty in strength of understanding.

AMP—Behold! God is mighty, and yet despises no one, nor regards anything as trivial; He is mighty in power of understanding and heart.

NIV—God is mighty, but does not despise men; he is mighty, and firm in his purpose.

Psalm 24:8

KJV—Who is this King of glory? The Lord strong and mighty, the Lord mighty in battle.

AMP—Who is the King of glory? The Lord, strong and mighty, the Lord, mighty in battle.

Moffatt—Who is the glorious King? 'Tis the Eternal, strong in might, the Eternal conquering from the fight.

Psalm 59:9

KJV—Because of his strength will I wait upon thee: for God is my defence.

NKJV—I will wait for You, O You his Strength; For God is my defense.

AMP—O my Strength, I will watch and give heed to You and sing praises; for God is my defense—my protector and high tower.

NAS—Because of his strength I will watch for Thee, For God is my stronghold.

Psalm 89:21-22

KJV—My hand shall be established: mine arm also shall strengthen him. The enemy shall not exact upon him; nor the son of wickedness afflict him.

AMP—My hand shall be established and ever abide, My arm also shall strengthen him. The enemy shall not exact from him or do him violence or outwit him, or the wicked afflict and humble him.

Moffatt—My hand shall always be a help to him, my arm shall make him strong; no foe shall ever surprise him, no miscreant shall master him.

NIV—My hand will sustain him; surely my arm will strengthen him. No enemy will subject him to tribute; no wicked man will oppress him.

Psalm 145:14

KJV—The Lord upholdeth all that fall, and raiseth up all those that be bowed down.

AMP—The Lord upholds all those [of His own] who are falling, and raises up all those who are bowed down.

Moffatt—The Eternal holds up any who are falling, and raises all who are bowed down.

NIV—The Lord upholds all those who fall and lifts up all who are bowed down.

John 17:1, 11, 14-15

KJV—These words spake Jesus, and lifted up his eyes to heaven, and said, Father... Keep through thine own name those whom thou hast given me, that they may be one, as we are. I have given them thy word; and the world hath hated them, because they are not of the world, even as I am not of the world. I pray not that thou shouldest take them out of the world, but that thou shouldest keep them from the evil.

NIV—After Jesus said this, he looked toward heaven and prayed: "Holy Father, protect them by the power of your name—the name you gave me—so that they may be one as we are one.... I have given them your word and the world has hated them, for they are not of the world any more than I am of the world. My prayer is not that you take them out of the world but that you protect them from the evil one."

*Never
Alone*

God's Contract
of Protection

*It shall come to pass, if thou
shalt hearken diligently unto the
voice of the Lord thy God, to observe
and to do all his commandments
which I command thee this day, that
the Lord thy God will set thee on
high above all nations of the earth....
The Lord shall cause thine enemies
that rise up against thee to be
smitten before thy face: they shall
come out against thee one way,
and flee before thee seven ways.*

Deuteronomy 28:1, 7

In the days to come you will see a great deal of trouble in the world around you. The reason is, there are two groups of people on the earth. There are the people of God and there are the people who still live in the devil's kingdom of darkness.

The Word of God tells us that these two groups, even though they may live side by side on the earth, will experience very different kinds of lives. We can see that in Isaiah 3 where the Lord tells Isaiah to "*say...to the righteous, that it shall be well with him.... Woe unto the wicked! it shall be ill with him*" (verses 10-11).

Take two groups of people living in the same space, in the same earth, in the same city, even in the same family, and one can live well and the other can live in woe. One can live in security and the other in constant peril. The difference is that one of these two groups has a covenant with God, and the other does not. God is a God of covenant, and God's covenant is a covenant of protection.

We see this in the preservation from their enemies that belonged to Israel, even before Jesus came and paid the price for man's sin. God made a way for His people to be secure. He said, "If you'll serve Me, if you'll obey Me, I'll be an enemy to your enemies and an adversary to your adversaries." And as long as Israel obeyed God no enemy could stand before them. No enemy could overrun them. No sickness and disease was in their midst. No catastrophe would come upon them if they lived with God. If they obeyed God and did what He said.

If the Israelites under the Old Covenant had that much protection, think how much protection belongs to those who are in Christ—who are in the One anointed to defeat Satan and restore to man the glory lost in the Fall. As good as those covenants were, God has made a new and better covenant with you through Jesus Christ, His Son. God has offered all He has—His Son, His Word, His Name, His Spirit, His Love—to you. Actually, you and I can walk in the comfort of the Holy Ghost every day. Think about that. The comfort, the protection, the counsel of the Spirit of God.

Don't let God's covenant sit on a shelf and gather dust. Use it for the peace and protection you and your family need in these troubled times.

His Commitment to Your Safety

Genesis 28:15

NKJV—I am with you and will keep you wherever you go.... I will not leave you until I have done what I have spoken to you.

AMP—I am with you, and will keep (watch over you with care, take notice of) you wherever you may go.... I will not leave you until I have done all of which I have told you.

Moffatt—I am with you, I will guard you wherever you go.... I will never leave you till I have done what I have promised you.

NIV—I am with you and will watch over you wherever you go.... I will not leave you until I have done what I have promised you.

Deuteronomy 28:1, 7

KJV—If thou shalt hearken diligently unto the voice of the Lord thy God, to observe and to do all his commandments which I command thee this day, that the Lord thy God will set thee on high above all nations of the earth.... The Lord shall cause thine enemies that rise up against thee to be smitten before thy face: they shall come out against thee one way, and flee before thee seven ways.

AMP—If you will listen diligently to the voice of the Lord your God, being watchful to do all His commandments which I command you this day, the Lord your God will set you high above all the nations of the earth.... The Lord shall cause your enemies who rise up against you to be defeated before your face; they shall come out against you one way, and flee before you seven ways.

Moffatt—If only you will listen carefully to what the Eternal your God orders, mindful to carry out all his commands which I enjoin upon you this day, then the Eternal your God will lift you high above all the nations of the earth.... The foes who attack you the Eternal will rout before you; they may assail you all together, but they shall fly before you in all directions.

NIV—If you fully obey the Lord your God and carefully follow all his commands I give you today, the Lord your God will set you high above all the nations on earth.... The Lord will grant that the enemies who rise up against you will be defeated before you. They will come at you from one direction but flee from you in seven.

1 Chronicles 16:15, 20-22

KJV—Be ye mindful always of his covenant; the word which he commanded to a thousand generations.... When they went from nation to nation, and from one kingdom to another people; He [the Lord] suffered no man to do them wrong: yea, he reproved kings for their sakes, Saying, Touch not mine anointed, and do my prophets no harm.

AMP—Be mindful of His covenant forever, the promise which He commanded and established to a thousand generations.... When they went from nation to nation, and from kingdom to another people, He allowed no man to do them wrong; yes, He reproved kings for their sakes, Saying,

Touch not My anointed, and do My prophets no harm.

Moffatt—Never forget his compact, the pledge he gave for a thousand generations... [They wandered] from one nation to another, and from realm to realm...he would not let a man oppress them, he would punish kings on their account, saying, "Never touch my chosen, my prophets never harm."

NIV—He remembers his covenant forever, the word he commanded, for a thousand generations... They wandered from nation to nation, from one kingdom to another. He allowed no man to oppress them; for their sake he rebuked kings: "Do not touch my anointed ones; do my prophets no harm."

Psalm 37:28

KJV—The Lord loveth judgment, and forsaketh not his saints; they are preserved for ever.

AMP—The Lord delights in justice and forsakes not His saints; they are preserved for ever.

Moffatt—The Eternal, who loves honesty, never forsakes his faithful band.

NIV—The Lord loves the just and will not forsake his faithful ones. They will be protected forever.

Psalm 95:7

KJV—He is our God; and we are the people of his pasture, and the sheep of his hand.

AMP—He is our God; and we are the people of His pasture, and the sheep of His hand.

Moffatt—The Eternal is our God, and we the people whom he shepherds.

NIV—He is our God and we are the people of his pasture, the flock under his care.

Isaiah 54:17

KJV—No weapon that is formed against thee shall prosper; and every tongue that shall rise against thee in judgment thou shalt condemn. This is the heritage of the servants of the Lord, and their righteousness is of me, saith the Lord.

AMP—No weapon that is formed against you shall prosper, and every tongue that shall rise against you in judgment you shall show to be in the wrong. This [peace, righteousness, security, triumph over opposition] is the heritage of the servants of the Lord [those in whom the ideal Servant of the Lord is reproduced]. This is the righteousness or the vindication which they obtain from Me—this is that which I impart to them as their justification—says the Lord.

Moffatt—No weapon forged against you shall succeed, no tongue raised against you shall win its plea. Such is the lot of the Eternal's servants; thus, the Eternal promises, do I maintain their cause.

TLB—No weapon turned against you shall succeed, and you will have justice against every courtroom lie. This is the heritage of the servants of the Lord. This is the blessing I have given you, says the Lord.

His Commitment to Your Long Life

Deuteronomy 5:16

KJV—Honour thy father and thy mother, as the Lord thy God hath commanded thee; that thy days may be prolonged, and that it may go well with thee.

AMP—Honor your father and your mother, as the Lord your God commanded you, that your days may be prolonged, and that it may go well with you.

Moffatt—Honour your father and your mother, as the Eternal your God has ordered you, that you may have a long life and that all may go well with you.

NIV—Honor your father and your mother, as the Lord your God has commanded you, so that you may live long and that it may go well with you.

Psalm 33:18-19

KJV—The eye of the Lord is upon them that fear him, upon them that hope in his mercy; To deliver their soul from death, and to keep them alive in famine.

AMP—The Lord's eye is upon those who fear Him—who revere and worship Him with awe; who wait for Him and hope in His mercy and loving-kindness, To deliver them from death, and keep them alive in famine.

Moffatt—The Eternal's eye rests on his worshippers, who rest their hopes upon his kindness, that he may rescue them from death, and during famine-days keep them alive.

NIV—The eyes of the Lord are on those who fear him, on those whose hope is in his unfailing love, to deliver them from death and keep them alive in famine.

Psalm 56:12-13

KJV—O God...thou hast delivered my soul from death: wilt not thou deliver my feet from falling, that I may walk before God in the light of the living?

AMP—O God...You have delivered my life from death, yes, and my feet from falling, that I may walk before God in the light of life and of the living.

Moffatt—O God...thou hast saved my life from death, my feet from stumbling, that I might live, ever mindful of God, in the sunshine of life.

NIV—O God...you have delivered me from death and my feet from stumbling, that I may walk before God in the light of life.

Psalm 66:8-9

KJV—O bless our God, ye people, and make the voice of his praise to be heard: Which holdeth our soul in life, and suffereth not our feet to be moved.

AMP—Bless our God, O peoples, give Him grateful thanks and make the voice of His praise to be heard, Who put and kept us among the living, and has not allowed our feet to slip.

Moffatt—Bless our God, O ye nations, sound his praise aloud, who keeps us safe in life, and never lets us come to grief.

NIV—Praise our God, O peoples, let the sound of his praise be heard; he has preserved our lives and kept our feet from slipping.

Psalm 68:19-20

NKJV—Blessed be the Lord, Who daily loads us with benefits, The God of our salvation! Selah. Our God is the God of salvation; And to God the Lord belong escapes from death.

AMP—Blessed be the Lord, Who bears our burdens and carries us day by day, even the God Who is our salvation! Selah [pause, and calmly think of that]! God is to us a God of deliverances and salvation, and to God, the Lord, belongs escape from death [setting us free].

NIV—Praise be to the Lord, to God our Savior, who daily bears our burdens. Selah. Our God is a God who saves; from the Sovereign Lord comes escape from death.

NAS—Blessed be the Lord, who daily bears our burden, The God who is our salvation. Selah. God is to us a God of deliverances; And to God the Lord belong escapes from death.

Psalm 91:16

KJV—With long life will I satisfy him, and show him my salvation.

Moffatt—I will satisfy him with long life, and let him see my saving care.

TLB—I will satisfy him with a full life and give him my salvation.

Psalm 94:17-18

NIV—Unless the Lord had given me help, I would soon have dwelt in the silence of death. When I said, "My foot is slipping," your love, O Lord, supported me.

KJV—Unless the Lord had been my help, my soul had almost dwelt in silence. When I said, My foot slippeth; thy mercy, O Lord, held me up.

AMP—Unless the Lord had been my help, I would soon have dwelt in [the land where is] silence. When I said, My foot is slipping, Your mercy and loving-kindness, O Lord, held me up.

Moffatt—If the Eternal had not been my help, I would have soon passed to the silent land. When I think my foot is slipping, thy goodness, O Eternal, holds me up.

40

Protection
Promises

Psalm 103:1-4

Moffatt—Bless the Eternal, O my soul, let all my being bless his sacred name; bless the Eternal, O my soul, remember all his benefits; he pardons all your sins, and all your sicknesses he heals, he saves your life from death.

KJV—Bless the Lord, O my soul: and all that is within me, bless his holy name. Bless the Lord, O my soul, and forget not all his benefits: Who forgiveth all thine iniquities; who healeth all thy diseases; Who redeemeth thy life from destruction.

AMP—Bless—affectionately, gratefully praise—the Lord, O my soul, and all that is [deepest] within me, bless His holy name! Bless—affectionately, gratefully praise—the Lord, O my soul, and forget not [one of] all His benefits, Who forgives [every one of] all your iniquities, Who heals [each of] all your diseases; Who redeems your life from the pit and corruption.

NIV—Praise the Lord, O my soul; all my inmost being, praise his holy name. Praise the Lord, O my soul, and forget not all his benefits—who forgives all your sins and heals all your diseases, who redeems your life from the pit.

His Commitment to Act in Love and Mercy

Deuteronomy 4:31

KJV—(For the Lord thy God is a merciful God;) he will not forsake thee, neither destroy thee, nor forget the covenant of thy fathers which he sware unto them.

Deuteronomy 7:8

KJV—Because the Lord loved you, and because he would keep the oath which he had sworn unto your fathers, hath the Lord brought you out with a mighty hand, and redeemed you out of the house of bondmen.

AMP—Because the Lord loves you, and because He would keep the oath which He had sworn to your fathers, the Lord has brought you out with a mighty hand, and redeemed you out of the house of bondage.

Moffatt—Because the Eternal loves you, because he meant to keep his oath to your fathers, that the Eternal has brought you out by sheer strength, rescuing you from that slave-pen.

NIV—Because the Lord loved you and kept the oath he swore to your forefathers that he brought you out with a mighty hand and redeemed you from the land of slavery.

Psalm 6:4

KJV—Return, O Lord, deliver my soul: oh save me for thy mercies' sake.

AMP—Return [to my relief], O Lord, deliver my life; save me for the sake of Your stead-fast love and mercies.

Moffatt—O thou Eternal, save my life once more; for thy love's sake, succour me.

NIV—Turn, O Lord, and deliver me; save me because of your unfailing love.

Psalm 17:7

KJV—Show thy marvellous lovingkindness, O thou that savest by thy right hand them which put their trust in thee from those that rise up against them.

AMP—Show Your marvelous loving-kindness, O You Who save by Your right hand those who trust and take refuge in You, from those who rise up against them.

Moffatt—Strong saviour, in thy kindness interpose, for those who shelter with thee from their foes.

NIV—Show the wonder of your great love, you who save by your right hand those who take refuge in you from their foes.

Psalm 32:10

KJV—Many sorrows shall be to the wicked: but he that trusteth in the Lord, mercy shall compass him about.

AMP—Many are the sorrows of the wicked, but he who trusts, relies on and confidently leans on the Lord shall be compassed about with mercy and with loving-kindness.

God's Contract of Protection

Moffatt—Many a pang falls to the ungodly, but he who trusts in the Eternal shall enjoy his favour.

NIV—Many are the woes of the wicked, but the Lord's unfailing love surrounds the man who trusts in him.

Psalm 40:11

KJV—Withhold not thou thy tender mercies from me, O Lord: let thy lovingkindness and thy truth continually preserve me.

AMP—Withhold not Your tender mercies from me, O Lord; let Your loving-kindness and Your truth continually preserve me!

Moffatt—Thou wilt not keep back from me thy mercy; thy love and faithfulness shall ever be my guard.

NIV—Do not withhold your mercy from me, O Lord; may your love and your truth always protect me.

Psalm 107:1-3

KJV—O give thanks unto the Lord, for he is good: for his mercy endureth for ever. Let the redeemed of the Lord say so, whom he hath redeemed from the hand of the enemy; And gathered them out of the lands, from the east, and from the west, from the north, and from the south.

AMP—O give thanks to the Lord for He is good, for His mercy and loving-kindness endure for ever! Let the redeemed of the Lord say so, whom He has delivered from the hand of the adversary, And gathered them out of the lands, from the east and from the west, from the north and from the...south.

Moffatt—Hallelujah! ˙Give thanks to the Eternal!—he is good, his kindness never fails!˝ Be this the song of the redeemed, redeemed by the Eternal from their foes, gathered from lands afar, from east and west, from north and south.

NIV—Give thanks to the Lord, for he is good; his love endures forever. Let the redeemed of the Lord say this—those he redeemed from the hand of the foe, those he gathered from the lands, from east and west, from north and south.

Isaiah 54:10

KJV—For the mountains shall depart, and the hills be removed; but my kindness shall not depart from thee, neither shall the covenant of my peace be removed, saith the Lord that hath mercy on thee.

AMP—Though the mountains should depart and the hills be shaken or removed, yet My love and kindness shall not depart from you, nor shall My covenant of peace and completeness be removed, says the Lord, Who has compassion on you.

Moffatt—Though mountains be removed, and hills be shaken, never shall my love leave you, my compact for your welfare shall stand firm: so promises the Eternal in his pity.

NIV—"Though the mountains be shaken and the hills be removed, yet my unfailing love for you will not be shaken nor my covenant of peace be removed," says the Lord, who has compassion on you.

His Commitment to Respond to His Name

Psalm 20:1

KJV—The Lord hear thee in the day of trouble; the name of the God of Jacob defend thee.

AMP—The Lord answer you in the day of trouble! The name of the God of Jacob set you up on high [and defend you].

Moffatt—On the day of trouble may the Eternal answer you, may Jacob's God, whom you invoke, protect you.

NIV—May the Lord answer you when you are in distress; may the name of the God of Jacob protect you.

Psalm 31:3

KJV—For thou art my rock and my fortress; therefore for thy name's sake lead me, and guide me.

AMP—Yes, You are my rock and my fortress; therefore for Your name's sake lead me and guide me.

Moffatt—For thou art my crag and castle. As thou art God, oh lead me, guide me.

NIV—Since you are my rock and my fortress, for the sake of your name lead and guide me.

Proverbs 18:10

KJV—The name of the Lord is a strong tower: the righteous runneth into it, and is safe.

AMP—The name of the Lord is a strong tower; the [consistently] righteous man—upright and in right standing with God—runs into it and is safe, high [above evil] and strong.

Moffatt—The Eternal is a tower of strength: good men run in and are secure.

NIV—The name of the Lord is a strong tower; the righteous run to it and are safe.

Joel 2:32

KJV—Whosoever shall call on the name of the Lord shall be delivered.

AMP—Whoever shall call on the name of the Lord shall be delivered and saved.

Moffatt—Every worshipper of the Eternal shall be saved.

NIV—Everyone who calls on the name of the Lord will be saved.

Zechariah 13:9

KJV—They shall call on my name, and I will hear them: I will say, It is my people: and they shall say, The Lord is my God.

Secure in Jesus

They shall cry unto
the Lord because
of the oppressors,
and he shall send
them a saviour, and
a great one, and he
shall deliver them.
Isaiah 19:20

*Behold, I give unto you power
to tread on serpents and scorpions,
and over all the power of the enemy:
and nothing shall by any means hurt you.*
Luke 10:19

Jesus gave Himself as the last sacrifice of the Old Covenant. He became the sacrificial lamb, offered upon the altar of the Cross for one reason: to defeat Satan.

The blood Jesus shed is protection for those who will receive it by faith. In Egypt, the Israelites who applied the blood of the sacrificial lamb to their doorposts were delivered from the death angel. How much greater is the protecting power of *"the precious blood of Christ...a lamb without blemish and without spot"* (1 Peter 1:19).

By His blood we are separated from every curse of the law of sin and death and given access to every promise of the Spirit of life (Romans 8:2). By His Spirit we have the same anointing power in which He *"went about doing good, and healing all that were oppressed of the devil"* (Acts 10:38).

Principalities and powers were spoiled in Jesus' victory over death. He destroyed the authority of the devil and every demon of hell, bringing them down to nothing and stripping from them the armor they had trusted in!

Moments later, He stepped out of that tomb and walked out of there and said, "All *power is given unto me in heaven and in earth*" (Matthew 28:18).

That's not where it ended either. He said, "Therefore you go into all the world. You take My Name. You lay hands on the sick and they'll recover. You cast out the devil. I whipped him; you go enforce it." (See Mark 16:15-18.)

How do we do it? Jesus said, "*If ye abide in me, and my words abide in you, ye shall ask what ye will, and it shall be done unto you*" (John 15:7). We abide in Him by filling ourselves with the Word so that we bring its promises and authority into every situation that comes before us.

The Word that you meditate on and act on concerning your protection is the Word that's alive in you and will perform all God sent it to do on your behalf. Just as we receive wholeness for our bodies through faith, we will walk in all the protection that is ours in Jesus' victory over our enemy, Satan, if we will believe God for it.

Resting in His Victory

Isaiah 9:6-7

KJV—Unto us a child is born, unto us a son is given: and the government shall be upon his shoulder: and his name shall be called Wonderful, Counsellor, The mighty God, The everlasting Father, The Prince of Peace. Of the increase of his government and peace there shall be no end, upon the throne of David, and upon his kingdom, to order it, and to establish it with judgment and with justice from henceforth even for ever. The zeal of the Lord of hosts will perform this.

NIV—To us a child is born, to us a son is given, and the government will be on his shoulders. And he will be called Wonderful Counselor, Mighty God, Everlasting Father, Prince of Peace. Of the increase of his government and peace there will be no end. He will reign on David's throne and over his kingdom, establishing and upholding it with justice and righteousness from that time on and forever. The zeal of the Lord Almighty will accomplish this.

AMP—To us a child is born, to us a son is given; and the government shall be upon His shoulder, and His name shall be called Wonderful Counselor, Mighty God, Everlasting Father (of Eternity), Prince of Peace. Of the increase of His government and of peace there shall be no end, upon the throne of David and over His kingdom, to establish it and to uphold it with justice and with righteousness from the latter time forth, even for evermore. The zeal of the Lord of hosts will perform this.

Isaiah 19:20

KJV—They shall cry unto the Lord because of the oppressors, and he shall send them a saviour, and a great one, and he shall deliver them.

AMP—They will cry to the Lord because of oppressors, and He will send them a savior, even a mighty one, and he will deliver them.

Moffatt—When any who are oppressed cry to the Eternal to send a champion, he will intervene and rescue them.

NIV—When they cry out to the Lord because of their oppressors, he will send them a savior and defender, and he will rescue them.

Luke 1:67-75

NKJV—Zacharias was filled with the Holy Spirit, and prophesied, saying: Blessed is the Lord God of Israel, For He has visited and redeemed His people, And has raised up a horn of salvation for us...As He spoke by the mouth of His holy prophets, Who have been since the world began, That we should be saved from our enemies And from the hand of all who hate us, To perform the mercy promised to our fathers And to remember His holy covenant, The oath which He swore to our father Abraham: To grant us that we, Being delivered from the hand of our enemies, Might serve Him without fear, In holiness and righteousness before Him all the days of our life.

Weymouth—Zechariah...was filled with the Holy Spirit, and he prophesied, saying,

"Blessed be the Lord, the God of Israel, Because He has not forgotten His people but has effected redemption for them, And has raised up a mighty Deliverer for us...As He has spoken from of old by the lips of His holy prophets—To deliver us from our foes and from the power of all who hate us, Dealing pitifully with our forefathers, And to remember His holy covenant, The oath which He swore to Abraham our forefather, To grant us to be rescued from the power of our foes And so render worship to Him free from fear, In holiness and uprightness before Him all our days."

Luke 10:19

AMP—Behold! I have given you authority and power to trample upon serpents and scorpions, and (physical and mental strength and ability) over all the power that the enemy [possesses], and nothing shall in any way harm you.

KJV—Behold, I give unto you power to tread on serpents and scorpions, and over all the power of the enemy: and nothing shall by any means hurt you.

Weymouth—I have given you power to tread serpents and scorpions under foot, and to trample on all the power of the enemy; and in no case shall anything do you harm.

NIV—I have given you authority to trample on snakes and scorpions and to overcome all the power of the enemy; nothing will harm you.

John 3:16-17

AMP—For God so greatly loved and dearly prized the world that He [even] gave up His only-begotten (unique) Son, so that whoever believes in (trusts, clings to, relies on) Him shall not perish—come to destruction, be lost—but have eternal (everlasting) life. For God did not send the Son into the world in order to judge—to reject, to condemn, to pass sentence on—the world; but that the world might find salvation and be made safe and sound through Him.

KJV—For God so loved the world, that he gave his only begotten Son, that whosoever believeth in him should not perish, but have everlasting life. For God sent not his Son into the world to condemn the world; but that the world through him might be saved.

NIV—For God so loved the world that he gave his one and only Son, that whoever believes in him shall not perish but have eternal life. For God did not send his Son into the world to condemn the world, but to save the world through him.

Pleading the Blood

Under the Old Covenant, the blood of an animal was shed as a picture of the coming of God's own Son to shed His blood for man's sin. Old Covenant sacrifices covered over the sin of God's covenant people, allowing them the right to stand in every promise of His covenant. Jesus' blood completely washes away the sin of the believer, allowing the believer to enjoy not only eternal salvation, but also every benefit of that salvation—including God's protection in the challenges of daily life. To every claim of the enemy's right to steal, kill and destroy, we plead the blood of Jesus and its power to separate us from every curse of sin and death.

Hebrews 10:19-22

KJV—Having therefore, brethren, boldness to enter into the holiest by the blood of Jesus, By a new and living way, which he hath consecrated for us, through the veil, that is to say, his flesh; And having an high priest over the house of God; Let us draw near with a true heart in full assurance of faith, having our hearts sprinkled from an evil conscience, and our bodies washed with pure water.

NKJV—Therefore, brethren, having boldness to enter the Holiest by the blood of Jesus, by a new and living way which He consecrated for us, through the veil, that is, His flesh, and having a High Priest over the house of God, let us draw near with a true heart in full assurance of faith, having our hearts sprinkled from an evil conscience and our bodies washed with pure water.

NIV—Therefore, brothers, since we have confidence to enter the Most Holy Place by the blood of Jesus, by a new and living way opened for us through the curtain, that is, his body, and since we have a great priest over the house of God, let us draw near to God with a sincere heart in full assurance of faith, having our hearts sprinkled to cleanse us from a guilty conscience and having our bodies washed with pure water.

Hebrews 13:12

KJV—Jesus also, that he might sanctify the people with his own blood, suffered without the gate.

NKJV—Jesus also, that He might sanctify the people with His own blood, suffered outside the gate.

NIV—Jesus also suffered outside the city gate to make the people holy through his own blood.

1 Peter 1:18-19

KJV—Forasmuch as ye know that ye were not redeemed with corruptible things, as silver and gold, from your vain conversation received by tradition from your fathers; But with the precious blood of Christ, as of a lamb without blemish and without spot.

NKJV—Knowing that you were not redeemed with corruptible things, like silver or gold, from your aimless conduct received by tradition from your fathers, but with the precious blood of Christ, as of a lamb without blemish and without spot.

NIV—For you know that it was not with perishable things such as silver or gold that you were redeemed from the empty way of life handed down to you from your forefathers, but with the precious blood of Christ, a lamb without blemish or defect.

Revelation 12:10-11

KJV—Now is come salvation, and strength, and the kingdom of our God, and the power of his Christ: for the accuser of our brethren is cast down, which accused them before our God day and night. And they overcame him by the blood of the Lamb, and by the word of their testimony.

AMP—Now it has come, the salvation and the power and the kingdom (the dominion, the reign) of our God and the power (the sovereignty, the authority) of His Christ, the Messiah; for the accuser of our brethren, he who keeps bringing before our God charges against them day and night, has been cast out! And they have overcome (conquered) him by means of the blood of the Lamb and by the utterance of their testimony.

Weymouth—Now is come the salvation and the power and the kingdom of our God, and the sovereignty of His Christ; for the accuser of our brethren has been hurled down—he who, day after day and night after night, was wont [accustomed] to accuse them in the presence of God. But they have gained the victory over him because of the blood of the Lamb and of the testimony which they have borne.

NIV—Now have come the salvation and the power and the kingdom of our God, and the authority of his Christ. For the accuser of our brothers, who accuses them before our God day and night, has been hurled down. They overcame him by the blood of the Lamb and by the word of their testimony.

Acting Confidently

Matthew 10:18-20

KJV—Ye shall be brought before governors and kings for my sake, for a testimony against them and the Gentiles. But when they deliver you up, take no thought how or what ye shall speak: for it shall be given you in that same hour what ye shall speak.

For it is not ye that speak, but the Spirit of your Father which speaketh in you.

John 16:13-15

KJV—Howbeit when he, the Spirit of truth, is come, he will guide you into all truth: for he shall not speak of himself; but whatsoever he shall hear, that shall he speak: and he will show you things to come. He shall glorify me: for he shall receive of mine, and shall show it unto you. All things that the Father hath are mine: therefore said I, that he shall take of mine, and shall show it unto you.

Acts 4:1-2, 18-21

KJV—And as they spake unto the people, the priests, and the captain of the temple, and the Sadducees, came upon them, Being grieved that they taught the people, and preached through Jesus the resurrection from the dead.... And they called them, and commanded them not to speak at all nor teach in the name of Jesus. But Peter and John answered and said unto them, Whether it be right in the sight of God to hearken unto you more than unto God, judge ye. For we cannot but speak the things which we have seen and heard. So when they had further threatened them, they let them go, finding nothing how they might punish them, because of the people: for all men glorified God for that which was done.

Acts 5:24-29

KJV—Now when the high priest and the captain of the temple and the chief priests heard these things, they doubted of them whereunto this would grow. Then came one and told them, saying, Behold, the men whom ye put in prison are standing in the temple, and teaching the people. Then went the captain with the officers, and brought them without violence: for they feared the people, lest they should have been stoned. And when they had brought them, they set them before the council: and the high priest asked them, Saying, Did not we straitly command you that ye should not teach in this name? and, behold, ye have filled Jerusalem with your doctrine, and intend to bring this man's blood upon us. Then Peter and the other apostles answered and said, We ought to obey God rather than men....

1 Peter 3:14-16

KJV—Be not afraid of their terror, neither be troubled; But sanctify the Lord God in your hearts: and be ready always to give an answer to every man that asketh you a reason of the hope that is in you with meekness and fear: Having a good conscience; that, whereas they speak evil of you, as of evildoers, they may be ashamed that falsely accuse your good conversation in Christ.

The Right
Place to Be

The righteous cry,
and the Lord heareth,
and delivereth them out
of all their troubles.
Psalm 34:17

He hath made him to be sin
for us, who knew no sin;
that we might be made the
righteousness of God in him.
2 Corinthians 5:21

Protection
Promises

God's mercy and lovingkindness are available in any situation to any man or woman who will by faith in His love cry out to Him. But the blessings of continual security and well-being belong to those who through faith walk in the promises God has made to those who are in right-standing with Him.

God's Word is filled with His promises to take care of those who are righteous: *"Say... to the righteous, that it shall be well with him"*... *"The eyes of the Lord are upon the righteous"*... *"The righteous cry, and the Lord heareth, and delivereth them out of all their troubles"*... *"There shall no evil happen to the just."* (See Isaiah 3:10; Psalm 34:15, 17; Proverbs 12:21.)

When we read the many scriptures that declare God's protection over the righteous, some think that means God protects people who are good and never do anything wrong. That's a misunderstanding of true righteousness that has kept many people from taking comfort in God's promises to them.

Righteousness is right-standing with God, and it comes in only one way—by the blood of the Lamb, Jesus, which was shed not just to cover but to completely remove man's sin. Second Corinthians 5:21 tells us God "*made him to be sin for us, who knew no sin; that we might be made the righteousness of God in him.*" Speaking prophetically of Jesus, Isaiah said God "*hath clothed me with the garments of salvation, he hath covered me with the robe of right-eousness, as a bridegroom decketh himself with ornaments, and as a bride adorneth herself with her jewels*" (Isaiah 61:10). Ephesians 4:24 instructs us to "*put on the new man, which after God is created in righteousness and true holiness.*"

To be righteous is to by faith accept that exchange made available to us at the cross—our unrighteousness for the right-eousness of Jesus Himself.

You can't get in any more right-standing with God than when you have made Jesus Christ the Lord of your life: "*Surely, shall one say, in the Lord have I righteousness and strength: even to him shall men come; and all that are incensed against him shall be ashamed*" (Isaiah 45:24).

Genesis 6:13-14, 17-19

KJV—And God said unto Noah, The end of all flesh is come before me; for the earth is filled with violence through them; and, behold, I will destroy them with the earth. Make thee an ark.... And, behold, I, even I, do bring a flood of waters upon the earth, to

destroy all flesh, wherein is the breath of
life, from under heaven; and every thing
that is in the earth shall die. But with thee
will I establish my covenant; and thou shalt
come into the ark, thou, and thy sons, and
thy wife, and thy sons' wives with thee. And
of every living thing of all flesh, two of
every sort shalt thou bring into the ark, to
keep them alive with thee.

Genesis 15:6

KJV—And he [Abram] believed in the Lord;
and he counted it to him for righteousness.

NIV—Abram believed the Lord, and he
credited it to him as righteousness.

AMP—And [Abram] believed, (trusted in,
relied on, remained steadfast to the Lord);
and He counted it to him as righteousness
[right standing with God.]

NKJV—And he [Abram] believed in the Lord,
and He accounted it to him for righteousness.

Psalm 7:10

KJV—My defence is of God, which saveth
the upright in heart.

AMP—My defense and shield depend on
God, Who saves the upright in heart.

Moffatt—God shields us, he who saves the
upright heart.

NIV—My shield is God Most High, who saves the upright in heart.

Psalm 34:15

KJV—The eyes of the Lord are upon the righteous, and his ears are open unto their cry.

AMP—The eyes of the Lord are toward the [uncompromisingly] righteous, and His ears are open to their cry.

NIV—The eyes of the Lord are on the righteous and his ears are attentive to their cry.

NAS—The eyes of the Lord are toward the righteous, And His ears are open to their cry.

Psalm 118:14-15

KJV—The Lord is my strength and song, and is become my salvation. The voice of rejoicing and salvation is in the tabernacles of the righteous.

AMP—The Lord is my strength and song, and He is become my salvation. The voice of rejoicing and salvation is in the tents and private dwellings of the [uncompromisingly] righteous.

Moffatt—The Eternal is my strength, of him I sing, he has delivered me indeed. Hark, the joyful shout of triumph in the tents of the just!

NIV—The Lord is my strength and my song; he has become my salvation. Shouts of joy and victory resound in the tents of the righteous.

Proverbs 11:8

KJV—The righteous is delivered out of trouble, and the wicked cometh in his stead.

AMP—The [uncompromisingly] righteous is delivered out of trouble, and the wicked gets into it instead.

Moffatt—The good man is brought safe out of adversity: the bad man takes his place!

NIV—The righteous man is rescued from trouble, and it comes on the wicked instead.

Isaiah 61:10

KJV—My soul shall be joyful in my God; for he hath clothed me with the garments of salvation, he hath covered me with the robe of righteousness, as a bridegroom decketh himself with ornaments, and as a bride adorneth herself with her jewels.

AMP—My soul shall exult in my God; for He has clothed me with the garments of salvation, He has covered me with the robe of righteousness, as a bridegroom decks himself with a garland, and as a bride adorns herself with her jewels.

NIV—My soul rejoices in my God. For he has clothed me with garments of salvation and arrayed me in a robe of righteousness, as a bridegroom adorns his head like a priest, and as a bride adorns herself with her jewels.

Isaiah 58:8

NKJV—Then your light shall break forth like the morning, Your healing shall spring forth speedily, And your righteousness shall go before you; The glory of the Lord shall be your rear guard.

AMP—Then shall your light break forth as the morning, and your healing [your restoration and the power of a new life] shall spring forth speedily; your righteousness [your rightness, your justice and your right relationship with God] shall go before you [conducting you to peace and prosperity], and the glory of the Lord shall be your rear guard.

NIV—Then your light will break forth like the dawn, and your healing will quickly appear; then your righteousness will go before you, and the glory of the Lord will be your rear guard.

NAS—Then your light will break out like the dawn, And your recovery will speedily spring forth; And your righteousness will go before you; The glory of the Lord will be your rear guard.

2 Corinthians 5:18, 21

KJV—God...hath reconciled us to himself by Jesus Christ.... For he hath made him to be sin for us, who knew no sin; that we might be made the righteousness of God in him.

AMP—God...through Jesus Christ reconciled us to Himself.... For our sake He made Christ [virtually] to be sin Who knew no sin, so that in and through Him we might become [endued with, viewed as in and examples of] the righteousness of God—what we ought to be, approved and acceptable and in right relationship with Him, by His goodness.

Weymouth—God...has reconciled us to Himself through Christ.... He has made Him who knew nothing of sin to be sin for us, in order that in Him we may become the righteousness of God.

NIV—God...reconciled us to himself through Christ.... God made him who had no sin to be sin for us, so that in him we might become the righteousness of God.

Galatians 3:6-7, 27

KJV—Abraham believed God, and it was accounted to him for righteousness. Know ye therefore that they which are of faith, the same are the children of Abraham.... For as many of you as have been baptized into Christ have put on Christ.

Protection
Promises

AMP—Abraham believed and adhered to and trusted in and relied on God, and it was reckoned and placed to his account and accredited as righteousness—as conformity to the divine will in purpose, thought and action. Know and understand that it is [really] the people [who live] by faith who are [the true] sons of Abraham.... For as many [of you] as were baptized into Christ—into a spiritual union and communion with Christ, the Anointed One, the Messiah—have put on (clothed yourselves with) Christ.

Weymouth—Abraham believed God, and it was placed to his account as righteousness. You see, then, that those who rest on faith are the true sons of Abraham.... For all of you who have been baptized into Christ have clothed yourselves with Christ.

NIV—Consider Abraham: "He believed God, and it was credited to him as righteousness." Understand, then, that those who believe are children of Abraham.... For all of you who were baptized into Christ have clothed yourselves with Christ.

Ephesians 4:22-24

KJV—Put off...the old man...And be renewed in the spirit of your mind; And...put on the new man, which after God is created in righteousness and true holiness.

AMP—Strip yourselves of your former nature—put off and discard your old unrenewed self...And be constantly renewed in the spirit of your mind—having a fresh mental and spiritual attitude; And put on the new nature (the regenerate self) created in God's image, (Godlike) in true righteousness and holiness.

Moffatt—Lay aside the old nature...and be renewed in the spirit of your mind, putting on the new nature, that divine pattern which has been created in the upright and pious character of the Truth.

NIV—Put off your old self...to be made new in the attitude of your minds; and to put on the new self, created to be like God in true righteousness and holiness.

Hebrews 11:7

AMP—[Prompted] by faith Noah, being forewarned of God concerning events of which as yet there was no visible sign, took heed and diligently and reverently constructed and prepared an ark for the deliverance of his own family. By this [his faith which relied on God] he passed judgment and sentence on the world's unbelief and became an heir and possessor of righteousness, [that relation of being right into which God puts the person who has faith].

NIV—By faith Noah, when warned about things not yet seen, in holy fear built an ark to save his family. By his faith he condemned the world and became heir of the righteousness that comes by faith.

NKJV—By faith Noah, being divinely warned of things not yet seen, moved with godly fear, prepared an ark for the saving of his household, by which he condemned the world and became heir of the righteousness which is according to faith.

KJV—By faith Noah, being warned of God of things not seen as yet, moved with fear, prepared an ark to the saving of his house; by the which he condemned the world, and became heir of the righteousness which is by faith.

Guided Safely
by God's Word

Get wisdom, get
understanding: forget it
not; neither decline from
the words of my mouth.
Forsake her not, and
she shall preserve thee:
love her, and she
shall keep thee.
Proverbs 4:5-6

Whosoever cometh to me, and
heareth my sayings, and doeth them,
I will show you to whom he is like:
He is like a man which built an house,
and digged deep, and laid the foundation
on a rock: and when the flood arose,
the stream beat vehemently upon
that house, and could not shake it:
for it was founded upon a rock.
Luke 6:47-48

Time after time, people get delivered out of seemingly impossible situations with one word from God. God's wisdom does make a difference, and He isn't keeping it hidden from us. In fact, Proverbs 1:20 says, "*Wisdom crieth without; she uttereth her voice in the streets.*" Verse 33 tells us what Wisdom is saying: "*Whoso hearkeneth unto me shall dwell safely, and shall be quiet from fear of evil.*"

Wisdom is not quiet. It's crying out to give us answers about how to walk in the ways of God that lead to His protection and provision. It's crying out with answers and instructions in our spirit that no man can know by his own reasoning. It's warning us of choices that can lead to danger.

How do you get the wisdom of God that will guide you safely through any situation? You get it by spending time in God's Word. In fact, Jesus referred to God's Word as the wisdom of God (Luke 11:49). Colossians 3:16 instructs us to *let the word of Christ dwell in you richly in all wisdom.*

God's wisdom and guidance by His Word and by His Spirit have been given to help us avoid the calamity and destruction that wait to come upon us like a whirlwind (Proverbs 1:25-27). Whether it is by a principle of living that helps us avoid danger, or the wisdom that enables us to confidently hear and respond to a prompting of the Spirit, God is always trying to give us the guidance that will lead us to safety. We will never take a wrong step when we follow the leading of God.

Make a lifestyle of thinking daily about the leading of God. Even when you can't take a long time to pray, practice every morning reminding God and reminding yourself: "I'm listening for You today, Father. I want You to talk to me." The devil isn't smart enough or subtle enough to sneak up and bring calamity or death on the believer who has learned how to walk in God's Word and hear His voice.

Find out His safe plans for you by reading and studying His Word. When you know God's plan, it's easy to go where He goes. God can handle anything that comes up. He can make everything work out. He can see ahead and He will guide you. Just

Guided Safely by God's Word

follow His steps. Stick with God's Word and He will stick to you like glue.

Preserved by His Word

1 Kings 11:38

KJV—If thou wilt hearken unto all that I command thee, and wilt walk in my ways, and do that is right in my sight, to keep my statutes and my commandments, as David my servant did; that I will be with thee, and build thee a sure house, as I built for David.

AMP—If you will hearken to all I command you, and will walk in My ways, and do right in My sight, keeping My statutes and My commandments, as David My servant did, I will be with you and build you a sure house, as I built for David.

NIV—If you do whatever I command you and walk in my ways and do what is right in my eyes by keeping my statutes and commands, as David my servant did, I will be with you. I will build you a dynasty as enduring as the one I built for David.

NAS—If you listen to all that I command you and walk in My ways, and do what is right in My sight by observing My statutes and My commandments, as My servant David did, then I will be with you and build you an enduring house as I built for David.

Psalm 119:98

KJV—Thy commandments hast made me wiser than mine enemies.

AMP—Your commandments make me wiser than my enemies.

Moffatt—Thy commands make me wiser than my foes.

NIV—Your commands make me wiser than my enemies.

Proverbs 2:6-8

NKJV—The Lord gives wisdom; From His mouth come knowledge and understanding; He stores up sound wisdom for the upright; He is a shield to those who walk uprightly; He guards the paths of justice, And preserves the way of His saints.

AMP—The Lord gives skillful and godly Wisdom; from His mouth come knowledge and understanding. He hides away sound and godly Wisdom and stores it for the righteous—those who are upright and in right standing with Him; He is a shield to those who walk uprightly and in integrity, That He may guard the paths of justice. Yes, He preserves the way of His saints.

Moffatt—It is the Eternal who supplies wisdom, from him come insight and knowledge, he has help ready for the upright, he is a shield for those who live honestly, a safeguard for the straight life, a protection for the pious.

NIV—The Lord gives wisdom, and from his mouth come knowledge and understanding. He holds victory in store for the upright, he is a shield to those whose walk is blameless, for he guards the course of the just and protects the way of his faithful ones.

Proverbs 2:11-13

KJV—Discretion shall preserve thee, understanding shall keep thee: To deliver thee from the way of the evil man, from the man that speaketh froward things; Who leave the paths of uprightness, to walk in the ways of darkness.

AMP—Discretion shall watch over you, understanding shall keep you; To deliver you from the way of evil and the evil man, from men who speak perverse things and are liars, Men who forsake the paths of uprightness to walk in the ways of darkness.

Moffatt—Good sense will take charge of you, sound judgment will keep you right, saving you from wicked courses, from the self-willed speech of men who leave the paths of right to follow some dark course.

NIV—Discretion will protect you, and understanding will guard you. Wisdom will save you from the ways of wicked men, from men whose words are perverse, who leave the straight paths to walk in dark ways.

Proverbs 4:4-6

KJV—Let thine heart retain my words: keep my commandments, and live. Get wisdom, get understanding: forget it not; neither decline from the words of my mouth. Forsake her not, and she shall preserve thee: love her, and she shall keep thee.

AMP—Let your heart hold fast my words; keep my commandments and live. Get skillful and godly Wisdom, get understanding—discernment, comprehension and interpretation; do not forget, and do not turn back from the words of my mouth. Forsake not [Wisdom] and she will keep, defend and protect you; love her and she will guard you.

Moffatt—Keep in mind what I say, do what I bid you, and you shall live, swerve not from my orders. Get sense, get knowledge, at any cost get knowledge—never leave her, and she will guard you, love her and she will take care of you.

NIV—Lay hold of my words with all your heart; keep my commands and you will live. Get wisdom, get understanding; do not forget my words or swerve from them. Do not forsake wisdom, and she will protect you; love her, and she will watch over you.

*Guided Safely
by God's Word*

Luke 6:47-48

KJV—Whosoever cometh to me, and heareth my sayings, and doeth them, I will show you to whom he is like: He is like a man which built an house, and digged deep, and laid the foundation on a rock: and when the flood arose, the stream beat vehemently upon that house, and could not shake it: for it was founded upon a rock.

AMP—Every one who comes to Me and listens to My words (in order to heed their teaching) and does them, I will show you what he is like: He is like a man building a house, who dug and went down deep, and laid a foundation upon the rock; and when a flood arose, the torrent broke against that house and could not shake or move it, because it had been securely built—founded on a rock.

Weymouth—If any one who comes to me, listens to my words and puts them in practice, I will show you whom he is like. He is like a man who built a house, dug deep and laid the foundation on the rock; and when a flood came, the torrent burst upon that house, but was unable to shake it, because it was securely built.

NAS—Everyone who comes to Me, and hears My words, and acts upon them, I will show you whom he is like: he is like a man building a house, who dug deep and laid a foundation upon the rock; and when a flood rose, the torrent burst against that house and could not shake it, because it had been well built.

Directed in Safe Paths

2 Samuel 22:29

KJV—Thou art my lamp, O Lord: and the Lord will lighten my darkness.

AMP—You, O Lord, are my lamp; the Lord lightens my darkness.

Moffatt—O Eternal! thou art my lamp, O Eternal, thou wilt make my darkness shine.

NIV—You are my lamp, O Lord; the Lord turns my darkness into light.

Psalm 17:1, 4-5

KJV—O Lord...by the word of thy lips I have kept me from the paths of the destroyer. Hold up my goings in thy paths, that my footsteps slip not.

AMP—O Lord...by the Word of Your lips I have avoided the ways of the violent—the paths of the destroyer. My steps have held closely to Your paths—to the tracks of the One Who has gone on before; my feet have not slipped.

NIV—O Lord...by the word of your lips I have kept myself from the ways of the violent. My steps have held to your paths; my feet have not slipped.

NAS—O Lord...by the word of Thy lips I have kept from the paths of the violent. My steps have held fast to Thy paths. My feet have not slipped.

Psalm 18:36

KJV—Thou hast enlarged my steps under me, that my feet did not slip.

AMP—You have given plenty of room for my steps under me, that my feet did not slip.

Moffatt—Thou has given me room to move, and a foothold sure!

NIV—You broaden the path beneath me, so that my ankles do not turn.

Psalm 23

KJV—The Lord is my shepherd; I shall not want. He maketh me to lie down in green pastures: he leadeth me beside the still waters. He restoreth my soul: he leadeth me in the paths of righteousness for his name's sake. Yea, though I walk through the valley of the shadow of death, I will fear no evil: for thou art with me; thy rod and thy staff they comfort me. Thou preparest a table before me in the presence of mine enemies: thou anointest my head with oil; my cup runneth over. Surely goodness and mercy shall follow me all the days of my life: and I will dwell in the house of the Lord for ever.

AMP—The Lord is my shepherd [to feed, guide and shield me]; I shall not lack. He makes me lie down in (fresh, tender) green pastures; He leads me beside the still and restful waters. He refreshes and restores my life—my self; He leads me in the paths of righteousness [uprightness and right standing with Him—not for my earning it, but] for His name's sake. Yes, though I walk through the [deep, sunless] valley of the shadow of death, I will fear or dread no evil; for You are with me; Your rod [to protect] and Your staff [to guide], they comfort me. You prepare a table before me in the presence of my enemies; You anoint my head with oil; my [brimming] cup runs over. Surely or only goodness, mercy and unfailing love shall follow me all the days of my life; and through the length of days the house of the Lord [and His presence] shall be my dwelling place.

Moffatt—The Eternal shepherds me, I lack for nothing; he makes me lie in meadows green, he leads me to refreshing streams, he revives life in me. He guides me by true paths, as he himself is true. My road may run through a glen of gloom, but I fear no harm, for thou art beside me; thy club, thy staff—they give me courage. Thou art my host, spreading a feast for me, while my foes have to look on! Thou hast poured oil upon my head, my cup is brimming over; yes, and all through my life Goodness and Kindness wait on me, the Eternal's guest within his household evermore.

NIV—The Lord is my shepherd, I shall not be in want. He makes me lie down in green pastures, he leads me beside quiet waters, he restores my soul. He guides me in paths of righteousness for his name's sake. Even though I walk through the valley of the shadow of death, I will fear no evil, for you are with me; your rod and your staff, they comfort me. You prepare a table before me in the presence of my enemies. You anoint my head with oil; my cup overflows. Surely goodness and love will follow me all the days of my life, and I will dwell in the house of the Lord forever.

Psalm 25:10

KJV—All the paths of the Lord are mercy and truth unto such as keep his covenant and his testimonies.

AMP—All the paths of the Lord are mercy and steadfast love, even truth and faithfulness are they for those who keep His covenant and His testimonies.

NIV—All the ways of the Lord are loving and faithful for those who keep the demands of his covenant.

NAS—All the paths of the Lord are lovingkindness and truth To those who keep His covenant and His testimonies.

Psalm 27:11-12

KJV—Teach me thy way, O Lord, and lead me in a plain path, because of mine enemies. Deliver me not over unto the will of mine enemies: for false witnesses are risen up against me, and such as breathe out cruelty.

AMP—Teach me Your way, O Lord, and lead me in a plain and even path because of my enemies—those who lie in wait for me. Give me not up to the will of my adversaries; for false witnesses have risen up against me; they breathe out cruelty and violence.

Moffatt—Teach me what is thy way, O thou Eternal, and lead me by a level road; let not my foes thwart me—leave me not to the fury of my foes, for false witnesses have started up against me, breathing injury to me.

NIV—Teach me your way, O Lord; lead me in a straight path because of my oppressors. Do not turn me over to the desire of my foes, for false witnesses rise up against me, breathing out violence.

Psalm 32:8

KJV—I will instruct thee and teach thee in the way which thou shalt go: I will guide thee with mine eye.

AMP—I, the Lord, will instruct you and teach you in the way you should go; I will counsel you with My eye upon you.

Moffatt—I will instruct you and teach you what is the road to take; I will give you counsel.

NIV—I will instruct you and teach you in the way you should go; I will counsel you and watch over you.

Psalm 37:23-24

KJV—The steps of a good man are ordered by the Lord: and he delighteth in his way. Though he fall, he shall not be utterly cast down: for the Lord upholdeth him with his hand.

AMP—The steps of a [good] man are directed and established of the Lord, when He delights in his way [and He busies Himself with his every step]. Though he fall, he shall not be utterly cast down, for the Lord grasps his hand in support and upholds him.

Moffatt—When a man's life pleases the Eternal, he gives him a sure footing; he may fall, but he never falls down, for the Eternal holds him by the hand.

NIV—If the Lord delights in a man's way, he makes his steps firm; though he stumble, he will not fall, for the Lord upholds him with his hand.

Psalm 73:20, 23-24

KJV—O Lord...I am continually with thee: thou hast holden me by my right hand. Thou shalt guide me with thy counsel.

AMP—O Lord...I am continually with You; You do hold my right hand. You will guide me with Your counsel.

Moffatt—[O Lord]...I am always beside thee; thou holdest my right hand, guiding me with thy counsel.

NIV—O Lord...I am always with you; you hold me by my right hand. You guide me with your counsel.

Psalm 121:1-8

KJV—I will lift up mine eyes unto the hills, from whence cometh my help. My help cometh from the Lord, which made heaven and earth. He will not suffer thy foot to be moved: he that keepeth thee will not slumber. Behold, he that keepeth Israel shall neither slumber nor sleep. The Lord is thy keeper: the Lord is thy shade upon thy right hand. The sun shall not smite thee by day, nor the moon by night. The Lord shall preserve thee from all evil: he shall preserve thy soul. The Lord shall preserve thy going out and thy coming in from this time forth, and even for evermore.

AMP—I will lift up my eyes to the hills [around Jerusalem to sacred Mount Zion and Mount Moriah]. From whence shall my help come? My help comes from the Lord, Who made Heaven and earth. He will not allow your foot to slip or to be moved; He Who keeps you will not slumber. Behold, He who keeps Israel will neither slumber nor sleep. The Lord is your keeper; the Lord is your shade on your right hand [the side not carrying a shield]. The sun shall not smite you by day, nor the moon by night. The Lord will keep you from all evil; He will keep your life. The Lord will keep your going out and your coming in from this time forth and for evermore.

Moffatt—I lift mine eyes to the mountains; ah, where is help to come from? Help comes from the Eternal who made heaven and earth. Never will he let you slip; he who guards you never sleeps: he who guards Israel will neither sleep nor slumber. The Eternal guards you, sheltering you upon the right; the sun shall never hurt you in the day, nor the moon by night. The Eternal will guard you from all harm, he will preserve your life; he will protect you as you come and go, now and for evermore.

Isaiah 45:1-2

KJV—Thus saith the Lord...I will go before thee, and make the crooked places straight.

AMP—Thus says the Lord...I will go before you and level the mountains—to make the crooked places straight.

Moffatt—Thus [says] the Eternal...I myself will go before you, levelling the mountains.

NAS—Thus says the Lord...I will go before you and make the rough places smooth.

Isaiah 48:17

NIV—This is what the Lord says—your Redeemer, the Holy One of Israel: "I am the Lord your God, who teaches you what is best for you, who directs you in the way you should go."

KJV—Thus saith the Lord, thy Redeemer, the Holy One of Israel; I am the Lord thy God which teacheth thee to profit, which leadeth thee by the way that thou shouldest go.

AMP—Thus says the Lord, your Redeemer, the Holy One of Israel: I am the Lord your God Who teaches you to profit, Who leads you by the way that you should go.

Moffatt—This is the word of the Eternal your deliverer, the Majestic One of Israel: I am the Eternal your God, training you for your good, leading you by the right way.

Jeremiah 31:9

KJV—They shall come with weeping, and with supplications will I lead them: I will cause them to walk by the rivers of waters in a straight way, wherein they shall not stumble: for I am a father to Israel.

AMP—They shall come with weeping [in penitence and for joy], and pouring out prayers [for the future]; I will lead them back; I will cause them to walk by streams of water, and bring them in a straight way in which they shall not stumble; for I am a father to Israel.

Moffatt—They went away in tears, but I lead them back consoled. I guide them to streams of water, by smooth roads where they cannot stumble; for to Israel I am a father.

NIV—They will come with weeping; they will pray as I bring them back. I will lead them beside streams of water on a level path where they will not stumble, because I am Israel's father.

John 16:13

KJV—When he, the Spirit of truth, is come, he will guide you into all truth: for he shall not speak of himself; but whatsoever he shall hear, that shall he speak: and he will show you things to come.

AMP—When He, the Spirit of Truth (the truth-giving Spirit) comes, He will guide you into all the truth—the whole, full truth. For He will not speak His own message—on His own authority—but He will tell whatever He hears [from the Father, He will give the message that has been given to Him] and He will announce and declare to you the things that are to come—that will happen in the future.

Weymouth—When He has come—the Spirit of truth—He will guide you into all the truth. For He will not speak of His own accord, but all that He hears He will speak, and He will make known the future to you.

NIV—When he, the Spirit of truth, comes, he will guide you into all truth. He will not speak on his own; he will speak only what he hears, and he will tell you what is yet to come.

Kept in a Protected Place

Psalm 18:27-33

KJV—Thou wilt save the afflicted people; but wilt bring down high looks. For thou wilt light my candle: the Lord my God will enlighten my darkness. For by thee I have run through a troop; and by my God have I leaped over a wall. As for God, His way is perfect: the word of the Lord is tried: he is a buckler to all those that trust in him. For who is God save the Lord? or who is a rock save our God? It is God that girdeth me with strength, and maketh my way perfect. He maketh my feet like hinds' feet, and setteth me upon my high places.

AMP—You deliver an afflicted and humble people, but will bring down haughty looks. For You cause my lamp to be lighted and shine; the Lord my God illumines my darkness. For by You I can run through a troop, and by my God I can leap over a wall. As for God, His way is perfect! The Word of the Lord is tested and tried; He is a shield to all those who take refuge and put their trust in Him. For who is God except the Lord? Or who is a rock save our God, The God who girds me with strength, and makes my way perfect? He makes my feet like hinds' feet [able to stand firmly or make progress on the dangerous heights of testing and trouble]; He sets me securely upon my high places.

Moffatt—The humble thou wilt raise, but the haughty thou wilt abase. O thou Eternal, thou wilt light my lamp, my God, thou wilt make my darkness shine; by thy help I can face a troop, by God's help I can leap a wall. God is unerring in his ways, the Eternal's promises are tried and true; he shields all who take shelter with him. For who is God save the Eternal? Who is steadfast but our God?—the God who girdles me with strength, and clears the path for me. He makes me nimble as a deer and sets me on the height.

NIV—You save the humble but bring low those whose eyes are haughty. You, O Lord, keep my lamp burning; my God turns my darkness into light. With your help I can advance against a troop; with my God I can scale a wall. As for God, his way is perfect; the word of the Lord is flawless. He is a shield for all who take refuge in him. For who is God besides the Lord? And who is the Rock except our God? It is God who arms me with strength and makes my way perfect. He makes my feet like the feet of a deer; he enables me to stand on the heights.

Psalm 25:4-5

KJV—Show me thy ways, O Lord; teach me thy paths. Lead me in thy truth, and teach me: for thou art the God of my salvation; on thee do I wait all the day.

AMP—Show me Your ways, O Lord; teach me Your paths. Guide me in Your truth and faithfulness and teach me, for You are the God of my salvation; for You [You only and altogether] do I wait (expectantly) all the day long.

NIV—Show me your ways, O Lord, teach me your paths; guide me in your truth and teach me, for you are God my Savior, and my hope is in you all day long.

NAS—Make me know Thy ways, O Lord; Teach me Thy paths. Lead me in Thy truth and teach me, For Thou art the God of my salvation; For Thee I wait all the day.

Psalm 25:20-21

KJV—O keep my soul, and deliver me: let me not be ashamed; for I put my trust in thee. Let integrity and uprightness preserve me; for I wait on thee.

AMP—O keep me, Lord, and deliver me; let me not be ashamed or disappointed, for my trust and my refuge are in You. Let integrity and uprightness preserve me, for I wait for and expect You.

Moffatt—Preserve me and deliver me; disappoint me not, as I take shelter with thee. May my devotion and my loyalty preserve me, for I am waiting for thyself, O thou Eternal.

NIV—Guard my life and rescue me; let me not be put to shame, for I take refuge in you. May integrity and uprightness protect me, because my hope is in you.

Psalm 31:1

KJV—In thee, O Lord, do I put my trust; let me never be ashamed: deliver me in thy righteousness.

AMP—In You, O Lord, do I put my trust and seek refuge; let me never be put to shame or [have my hope in You] disappointed; deliver me in Your righteousness!

Moffatt—With thee, O thou Eternal, I take shelter, never let me be disappointed; oh rescue me, as thou art faithful.

NIV—In you, O Lord, I have taken refuge; let me never be put to shame; deliver me in your righteousness.

Psalm 31:3-6

KJV—Lead me, and guide me. Pull me out of the net that they have laid privily for me: for thou art my strength. Into thine hand I commit my spirit: thou hast redeemed me, O Lord God of truth.... I trust in the Lord.

Guided Safely by God's Word

AMP—Lead me and guide me. Draw me out of the net that they have laid secretly for me; for You are my strength and my stronghold. Into Your hand I commit my spirit; You have redeemed me, O Lord God of truth and faithfulness.... I trust, rely on and confidently lean on the Lord.

Moffatt—Lead me, guide me, safe from the snares spread cunningly to catch me. Thou art my stronghold, I put my life into thy hands; and, O Eternal, O thou faithful God, thou savest me.... In the Eternal I do put my faith.

NIV—Lead and guide me. Free me from the trap that is set for me, for you are my refuge. Into your hands I commit my spirit; redeem me, O Lord, the God of truth.... I trust in the Lord.

Psalm 31:23-24

KJV—Love the Lord, all ye his saints: for the Lord preserveth the faithful, and plentifully rewardeth the proud doer. Be of good courage, and he shall strengthen your heart, all ye that hope in the Lord.

AMP—Love the Lord, all you His saints; the Lord preserves the faithful, and plentifully pays back him who deals haughtily. Be strong and let your heart take courage, all you who wait and hope for and expect the Lord!

Moffatt—Love the Eternal, all ye faithful; the Eternal will keep faith with you, and richly requite arrogant men. Only be strong, be brave, all ye who wait for the Eternal.

NIV—Love the Lord, all his saints! The Lord preserves the faithful, but the proud he pays back in full. Be strong and take heart, all you who hope in the Lord.

Psalm 40:1-2

KJV—I waited patiently for the Lord; and he inclined unto me, and heard my cry. He brought me up also out of an horrible pit, out of the miry clay, and set my feet upon a rock, and established my goings.

AMP—I waited patiently and expectantly for the Lord, and He inclined to me and heard my cry. He drew me up out of a horrible pit—a pit of tumult and of destruction—out of the miry clay (froth and slime) and set my feet upon a rock, steadying my steps and establishing my goings.

Moffatt—As patiently I waited for the Eternal, he turned and listened to my cry; he raised me from a lonesome pit, a muddy bog, he set my foot on a rock and steadied my steps.

NIV—I waited patiently for the Lord; he turned to me and heard my cry. He lifted me out of the slimy pit, out of the mud and mire; he set my feet on a rock and gave me a firm place to stand.

Psalm 125:1-2

KJV—They that trust in the Lord shall be as mount Zion, which cannot be removed, but abideth for ever. As the mountains are round about Jerusalem, so the Lord is round about his people from henceforth even for ever.

AMP—Those who trust, lean on and confidently hope in the Lord are as Mount Zion, which cannot be moved, but abides and stands fast for ever. As the mountains are round about Jerusalem, so the Lord is round about His people from this time forth and for ever.

Moffatt—Those who trust in the Eternal are like Sion hill, never to be shaken; Jerusalem sits enthroned for ever, with the hills around her, and the Eternal is around his people now and evermore.

NIV—Those who trust in the Lord are like Mount Zion, which cannot be shaken but endures forever. As the mountains surround Jerusalem, so the Lord surrounds his people both now and forevermore.

Psalm 128:1-2

KJV—Blessed is every one that feareth the Lord; that walketh in his ways. For thou shalt eat the labour of thine hands: happy shalt thou be, and it shall be well with thee.

AMP—Blessed—happy, fortunate |to be envied|—is every one who fears, reveres and worships the Lord; who walks in His ways and lives according to His commandments. For you shall eat |the fruit| of the labor of your hands; happy, blessed, fortunate |enviable| shall you be, and it shall be well with you.

NIV—Blessed are all who fear the Lord, who walk in his ways. You will eat the fruit of your labor; blessings and prosperity will be yours.

NAS—How blessed is everyone who fears the Lord, Who walks in His ways. When you shall eat of the fruit of your hands, You will be happy and it will be well with you.

2 Thessalonians 3:3

KJV—The Lord is faithful, who shall stablish you, and keep you from evil.

AMP—The Lord is faithful and He will strengthen [you] and set you on a firm foundation and guard you from the evil [one].

Weymouth—The Lord is faithful, and He will confirm and will guard you from the Evil One.

NIV—The Lord is faithful, and he will strengthen and protect you from the evil one.

Equipped to Hear God's Voice

Isaiah 30:21

KJV—Thine ears shall hear a word behind thee, saying, This is the way, walk ye in it, when ye turn to the right hand, and when ye turn to the left.

NIV—Whether you turn to the right or to the left, your ears will hear a voice behind you, saying, "This is the way; walk in it."

Moffatt—When you swerve to right or left, you hear a Voice behind you whispering, "This is the way, walk here."

TLB—If you leave God's paths and go astray, you will hear a Voice behind you say, "No, this is the way; walk here."

John 10:3-5

KJV—The sheep hear his voice: and he calleth his own sheep by name, and leadeth them out. And when he putteth forth his own sheep, he goeth before them, and the sheep follow him: for they know his voice. And a stranger will they not follow, but will flee from him: for they know not the voice of strangers.

AMP—The sheep listen to his voice and heed it, and he calls his own sheep by name and brings (leads) them out. When he has brought his own sheep outside, he walks on before them, and the sheep follow him, because they know his voice. They will never [on any account] follow a stranger, but will run away from him, because they do not know the voice of strangers or recognize their call.

Weymouth—The sheep hear his voice; and he calls his own sheep by their names and leads them out. When he has brought his own sheep all out, he walks at the head of them; and the sheep follow him, because they know his voice. But a stranger they will by no means follow, but will run away from him, because they do not know the voice of strangers.

NIV—The sheep listen to his voice. He calls his own sheep by name and leads them out. When he has brought out all his own, he goes on ahead of them, and his sheep follow him because they know his voice. But they will never follow a stranger; in fact, they will run away from him because they do not recognize a stranger's voice.

Given Words of Power

Psalm 91:2

NIV—I will *say* of the Lord, "He is my refuge and my fortress, my God, in whom I trust."

KJV—I will *say* of the Lord, He is my refuge and my fortress: my God; in him will I trust.

AMP—I will *say* of the Lord, He is my refuge and my fortress, my God, on Him I lean and rely, and in Him I (confidently) trust!

TLB—This I *declare*, that he alone is my refuge, my place of safety; he is my God, and I am trusting him.

Proverbs 4:20-24

KJV—My son, attend to my words; incline thine ear unto my sayings. Let them not depart from thine eyes; keep them in the midst of thine heart. For they are life unto those that find them, and health to all their flesh. Keep thy heart with all diligence; for out of it are the issues of life. Put away from thee a froward mouth, and perverse lips put far from thee.

AMP—My son, attend to my words; consent and submit to my sayings. Let them not depart from your sight; keep them in the center of your heart. For they are life to those who find them, healing and health to all their flesh. Keep your heart with all

Guided Safely by God's Word

vigilance and above all that you guard, for out of it flow the springs of life. Put away from you false and dishonest speech, and willful and contrary talk put far from you.

Moffatt—My son, attend to what I say, bend your ear to my words; never lose sight of them, but fix them in your mind; to those who find them, they are life, and health to all their being. Guard above all things, guard your inner self, for so you live and prosper; bar out all talk of evil, and banish wayward words.

NIV—My son, pay attention to what I say; listen closely to my words. Do not let them out of your sight, keep them within your heart; for they are life to those who find them and health to a man's whole body. Above all else, guard your heart, for it is the wellspring of life. Put away perversity from your mouth; keep corrupt talk far from your lips.

Proverbs 12:6

KJV—The mouth of the upright shall deliver them.

AMP—The mouth of the upright shall deliver them and the innocent ones [thus endangered].

NIV—The speech of the upright rescues them.

Mark 11:22-24

KJV—And Jesus answering saith unto them, Have faith in God. For verily I say unto you,

That whosoever shall *say* unto this mountain, Be thou removed, and be thou cast into the sea; and shall not doubt in his heart, but shall believe that those things which he *saith* shall come to pass; he shall have whatsoever he *saith*. Therefore I say unto you, What things soever ye desire, when ye pray, believe that ye receive them, and ye shall have them.

Luke 21:15, 18

KJV—I will give you a mouth and wisdom, which all your adversaries shall not be able to gainsay nor resist.... But there shall not an hair of your head perish.

AMP—I [Myself] will give you a mouth and such utterance and wisdom as all of your foes combined will be unable to stand against or refute.... But not a hair of your head shall perish.

Weymouth—I will give you utterance and wisdom which none of your opponents will be able to withstand or reply to.... Yet not a hair of your heads shall perish.

NIV—I will give you words and wisdom that none of your adversaries will be able to resist or contradict.... But not a hair of your head will perish.

Ephesians 6:17-18

KJV—Take the helmet of salvation, and the sword of the Spirit, which is the word of

God: Praying always with all prayer and supplication in the Spirit, and watching thereunto with all perseverance and supplication for all saints.

AMP—Take the helmet of salvation and the sword the Spirit wields, which is the Word of God. Pray at all times—on every occasion, in every season—in the Spirit, with all [manner of] prayer and entreaty. To that end keep alert and watch with strong purpose and perseverance, interceding in behalf of all the saints (God's consecrated people).

Weymouth—Receive the helmet of salvation, and the sword of the Spirit which is the word of God. Pray with unceasing prayer and entreaty at all times in the Spirit, and be always on the alert to seize opportunities for doing so, with unwearied persistence and entreaty on behalf of all the saints.

NIV—Take the helmet of salvation and the sword of the Spirit, which is the word of God. And pray in the Spirit on all occasions with all kinds of prayers and requests. With this in mind, be alert and always keep on praying for all the saints.

Caused to Sleep in Peace

Psalm 3:3-5

AMP—You, O Lord, are a shield for me, my glory, and the lifter up of my head. With my voice I cry to the Lord, and He hears and answers me out of His holy hill. Selah [pause, and calmly think of that]! I lay down and slept; I wakened again, for the Lord sustains me.

KJV—Thou, O Lord, art a shield for me; my glory, and the lifter up of mine head. I cried unto the Lord with my voice, and he heard me out of his holy hill. Selah. I laid me down and slept; I awaked; for the Lord sustained me.

Moffatt—Thou shieldest me, O thou Eternal, in triumph, thou whom I do glorify! When I call out to the Eternal, he answers me from his sacred hill. I laid me down to sleep, and this morning I waken, for the Eternal upholds me.

NIV—You are a shield around me, O Lord; you bestow glory on me and lift up my head. To the Lord I cry aloud, and he answers me from his holy hill. Selah. I lie down and sleep; I wake again, because the Lord sustains me.

Psalm 4:8

KJV—I will both lay me down in peace, and sleep: for thou, Lord, only makest me dwell in safety.

AMP—In peace I will both lie down and sleep, for You, Lord, alone make me dwell in safety and confident trust.

Moffatt—Quietly I lay me down to sleep, for even alone, thanks to thee, I am secure.

NIV—I will lie down and sleep in peace, for you alone, O Lord, make me dwell in safety.

Proverbs 3:21-24

KJV—Keep sound wisdom and discretion: So shall they be life unto thy soul, and grace to thy neck. Then shalt thou walk in thy way safely, and thy foot shall not stumble. When thou liest down, thou shalt not be afraid: yea, thou shalt lie down, and thy sleep shall be sweet.

AMP—Keep sound wisdom and discretion, And they will be life to your inner self, and a gracious ornament to your neck [your outer self]. Then you will walk on your way securely and in confident trust, and [you] shall not dash your foot or stumble. When you lie down you shall not be afraid; yes, you shall lie down and your sleep shall be sweet.

NIV—Preserve sound judgment and discernment, do not let them out of your sight; they will be life for you, an ornament to grace your neck. Then you will go on your way in safety, and your foot will not stumble; when you lie down, you will not be afraid; when you lie down, your sleep will be sweet.

NAS—Keep sound wisdom and discretion, So they will be life to your soul, And adornment to your neck. Then you will walk in your way securely, And your foot will not stumble. When you lie down, you will not be afraid; When you lie down, your sleep will be sweet.

Mark 4:37-41

KJV—There arose a great storm of wind, and the waves beat into the ship, so that it was now full. And he [Jesus] was in the hinder part of the ship, asleep on a pillow: and they awake him, and say unto him, Master, carest thou not that we perish?

And he arose, and rebuked the wind, and said unto the sea, Peace, be still. And the wind ceased, and there was a great calm. And he said unto them, Why are ye so fearful? how is it that ye have no faith?

And they feared exceedingly, and said one to another, What manner of man is this, that even the wind and the sea obey him?

AMP—A furious storm of wind (of hurricane proportions) arose, and the waves kept beating into the boat, so that it was already becoming filled. But He [Himself] was in the stern [of the boat] asleep on the [leather] cushion; and they awoke Him and said to Him, Master, do You not care that we are perishing?

And He arose and rebuked the wind, and said to the sea, Hush now! Be still (muzzled)! And the wind ceased, [that is, sank to rest as if exhausted by its beating] and there was (immediately) a great calm—a perfect peacefulness. He said to them, Why are you so timid and fearful? How is it that you have no faith—no firmly relying trust?

And they were filled with great awe and feared exceedingly and said to one another, Who then is this, that even wind and sea obey Him?

Weymouth—A heavy squall came on, and the waves were now dashing into the boat, so that it was fast filling. But He Himself was in the stern asleep, with His head on the cushion: so they woke Him. "Rabbi," they cried, "is it nothing to you that we are drowning?"

So He roused Himself and rebuked the wind, and said to the waves, "Silence! Be still!" The wind sank, and there was perfect calm. "Why are you so timid?" He asked; "have you still no faith?"

Then they were filled with terror, and began to say to one another, "Who then is this? For even wind and sea obey Him."

Chapter 6

Hidden in God

*O Lord, you bless
the righteous;
you surround them
with your favor
as with a shield.*
Psalm 5:12, NIV

*He that dwelleth in the secret place of the
most High shall abide under the shadow
of the Almighty. I will say of the Lord,
He is my refuge and my fortress:
my God; in him will I trust....
He shall cover thee with his feathers,
and under his wings shalt thou trust: his
truth shall be thy shield and buckler.*
Psalm 91:1-2, 4

No matter where you live, there are no safe places anymore in this earth. No matter where you go there is no security outside of God. But as believers, we have security everywhere we go because God is looking after us. He's our shield, our fortress, our refuge.

Absolute safety belongs to the one who says of the Lord, "*He is my refuge and my fortress.*" That is the one of whom David said, "*He shall cover thee with his feathers, and under his wings shalt thou trust; his truth shall be thy shield and buckler. Thou shalt not be afraid...*" (Psalm 91:4-5).

To live free while you're here in the earth, you must know the truth of God's covenant promises to you in Christ, and use that truth like a shield and a buckler.

How do you use the truth like a shield and a buckler? By trusting in it. By being steadfast in your faith and by staying in the Word every day. Proverbs 18:10 in *The Amplified Bible* says, "*The name of the Lord is a strong tower; the [consistently] righteous man— upright and in right standing with God—runs into it and is safe, high [above evil] and strong.*"

When you stay in God's Word consistently, His words will become the first things that come to your mind in any situation so you can speak them out in faith. His promises will rise up within you in times of trouble and be the shield, fortress or refuge you need.

When events in the world start to look dark and troubled, don't be moved by the things that are going on around you. Remember, instead, that God has the ability, the wonderful ability, to deliver you.

Your Only Salvation

Deuteronomy 33:26-27

NKJV—There is no one like the God of Jeshurun [Israel], Who rides the heavens to help you, And in His excellency on the clouds. The eternal God is your refuge, And underneath are the everlasting arms.

AMP—There is none like God...Who rides through the heavens to your help, and in His majestic glory through the sky. The eternal God is your refuge and dwelling place, and underneath are the everlasting arms.

NIV—There is no one like the God of
Jeshurun [Israel], who rides on the heavens
to help you and on the clouds in his majesty.
The eternal God is your refuge, and underneath are the everlasting arms.

TLB—There is none like the God of
Jerusalem—He descends from the heavens
In majestic splendor to help you. The
eternal God is your Refuge, And underneath are the everlasting arms.

Proverbs 21:30-31

KJV—There is no wisdom nor understanding nor counsel against the Lord...safety is
of the Lord.

AMP—There is no wisdom or understanding
or counsel [that can prevail] against the
Lord...deliverance and victory are of the Lord.

Moffatt—Intelligence, skill, strategy—none
can avail against the Eternal...saving victory
comes from the Eternal.

NIV—There is no wisdom, no insight, no
plan that can succeed against the Lord...
victory rests with the Lord.

Isaiah 44:8

KJV—Fear ye not, neither be afraid: have
not I told thee from that time, and have
declared it? ye are even my witnesses. Is

there a God beside me? yea, there is no God; I know not any.

AMP—Fear not, nor be afraid [in the coming violent upheavals]; have I not told it to you from of old and declared it? And you are My witnesses! Is there a God besides Me? There is no other Rock; I know not any.

Moffatt—Fear nothing, dread not in the days to come; have I not foretold it and announced it long ago? You are my witnesses whether there is any god, any Power, any, besides me.

NIV—Do not tremble, do not be afraid. Did I not proclaim this and foretell it long ago? You are my witnesses. Is there any God besides me? No, there is no other Rock; I know not one.

Jeremiah 42:11-12

KJV—Be not afraid...saith the Lord: for I am with you to save you, and to deliver you.... And I will show mercies unto you.

AMP—Be not afraid...says the Lord, for [...the all-wise, all-powerful, and ever-present God] I, [the Lord] am with you to save you and to deliver you.... And I will grant mercy to you.

Moffatt—Never fear...the Eternal says, for I will be with you to rescue you.... I will have pity on you.

NIV—Do not be afraid...declares the Lord, for I am with you and will save you and deliver you.... I will show you compassion.

John 16:33

KJV—These things I have spoken unto you, that in me ye might have peace. In the world ye shall have tribulation: but be of good cheer; I have overcome the world.

AMP—I have told you these things so that in Me you may have perfect peace and confidence. In the world you have tribulation and trials and distress and frustration; but be of good cheer—take courage, be confident, certain, undaunted—for I have overcome the world.—I have deprived it of power to harm, have conquered it [for you].

Weymouth—I have spoken all this to you in order that in me you may have peace. In the world you have affliction. But keep up your courage: I have won the victory over the world.

NIV—I have told you these things, so that in me you may have peace. In this world you will have trouble. But take heart! I have overcome the world.

Galatians 1:3-4

KJV—Our Lord Jesus Christ...gave himself for our sins, that he might deliver us from this present evil world, according to the will of God and our Father.

AMP—Our Lord Jesus Christ, the Messiah... gave (yielded) Himself up [to atone] for our sins (and to save and sanctify us), in order to rescue and deliver us from this present wicked age and world order, in accordance with the will and purpose and plan of our God and Father.

Weymouth—Our Lord Jesus Christ...gave Himself for our sins in order to rescue us from the present wicked world in accordance with the will of our God and Father.

NIV—The Lord Jesus Christ...gave himself for our sins to rescue us from the present evil age, according to the will of our God and Father.

Your Hiding Place

Job 1:9-10

KJV—Satan answered the Lord, and said, Doth Job fear God for nought? Hast not thou made an hedge about him, and about his house, and about all that he hath on every side? thou hast blessed the work of his hands, and his substance is increased in the land.

AMP—Satan answered the Lord, Does Job (reverently) fear God for nothing? Have You not put a hedge about him and his house and all that he has, on every side? You have conferred prosperity and happiness upon him in the work of his hands, and his possessions have increased in the land.

Moffatt—The Adversary answered, "But is it for nothing that Eyob reverences God? Have you not hedged him safely in, his house and all he has? You have prospered him in his business, and his flocks are teeming on the land."

NIV—"Does Job fear God for nothing?" Satan replied. "Have you not put a hedge around him and his household and everything he has? You have blessed the work of his hands, so that his flocks and herds are spread throughout the land."

Psalm 17:6, 8-9

KJV—O God...Keep me as the apple of the eye, hide me under the shadow of thy wings, From the wicked that oppress me, from my deadly enemies, who compass me about.

AMP—O God...Keep and guard me as the pupil of the eye; hide me in the shadow of Your wings, From the wicked who despoil and oppress me, my deadly adversaries who surround me.

Moffatt—O God...guard us as thine own eye, hide us under the shadow of thy wings, from the ungodly who would harry us, the eager enemies that encircle us.

NIV—O God...Keep me as the apple of your eye; hide me in the shadow of your wings from the wicked who assail me, from my mortal enemies who surround me.

Psalm 27:5

KJV—In the time of trouble he shall hide me in his pavilion: in the secret of his tabernacle shall he hide me; he shall set me up upon a rock.

AMP—In the day of trouble He will hide me in His shelter; in the secret place of His tent will He hide me; He will set me high upon a rock.

Moffatt—He hides me within his own pavilion on the day of trouble, he shelters me within his shrine, he sets me safe upon a rock.

NIV—In the day of trouble he will keep me safe in his dwelling; he will hide me in the shelter of his tabernacle and set me high upon a rock.

Psalm 31:19-20

KJV—How great is thy goodness, which thou hast laid up for them that fear thee; which thou hast wrought for them that trust in thee before the sons of men! Thou shalt hide them in the secret of thy presence from the pride of man: thou shalt keep them secretly in a pavilion from the strife of tongues.

Hidden in God

AMP—How great is Your goodness, which You have laid up for those who fear, revere and worship You, goodness which You have wrought for those who trust and take refuge in You before the sons of men! In the secret of Your presence You hide them from the plots of men; You keep them secretly in Your pavilion from the strife of tongues.

Moffatt—What wealth of kindness thou hast laid up for thy worshippers, and shown to those who shelter with thyself! Thou hidest them under thy wings from human plots, thou shelterest them from the scourge of slander!

NIV—How great is your goodness, which you have stored up for those who fear you, which you bestow in the sight of men on those who take refuge in you. In the shelter of your presence you hide them from the intrigues of men; in your dwelling you keep them safe from accusing tongues.

Psalm 32:7

KJV—Thou art my hiding place; thou shalt preserve me from trouble; thou shalt compass me about with songs of deliverance.

AMP—You are a hiding place for me; You, Lord, preserve me from trouble; You surround me with songs and shouts of deliverance.

Moffatt—Thou wilt be his shelter, safeguarding him in peril, surrounding him with aid.

NIV—You are my hiding place; you will protect me from trouble and surround me with songs of deliverance.

Psalm 57:1

KJV—In the shadow of thy wings will I make my refuge, until these calamities be overpast.

AMP—In the shadow of Your wings will I take refuge and be confident until calamities and destructive storms are passed.

Moffatt—In the shadow of thy wings I shelter, till the deadly danger passes.

NIV—I will take refuge in the shadow of your wings until the disaster has passed.

Psalm 61:4

KJV—I will abide in thy tabernacle for ever: I will trust in the covert of thy wings.

AMP—I will dwell in Your tabernacle for ever; let me find refuge and trust in the shelter of Your wings.

Moffatt—Oh to be a guest of thine for ever! oh to be sheltered underneath thy wings!

NIV—I long to dwell in your tent forever and take refuge in the shelter of your wings.

Psalm 64:1-2

KJV—O God...Hide me from the secret counsel of the wicked; from the insurrection of the workers of iniquity.

Hidden in God

AMP—O God...Hide me from the secret counsel and conspiracy of the ungodly, from the scheming of evildoers.

Moffatt—O God...hide me from villains and their plots, from gangs of evildoers.

NIV—O God...Hide me from the conspiracy of the wicked, from that noisy crowd of evildoers.

Your Place of Refuge

2 Samuel 22:2-3

KJV—The Lord is my rock, and my fortress, and my deliverer; The God of my rock; in him will I trust: he is my shield, and the horn of my salvation, my high tower, and my refuge, my saviour; thou savest me from violence.

AMP—The Lord is my rock...and my fortress [in the wilderness] and my deliverer; My God, my rock; in Him will I take refuge; my shield, and the horn of my salvation, my stronghold, and my refuge, my savior; You save me from violence.

Moffatt—The Eternal is my crag, my stronghold, my deliverer—he is mine, my God, my fortalice where I take shelter, my shield, my saving strength, my refuge and retreat, my rescue from the violent.

NIV—The Lord is my rock, my fortress and my deliverer; my God is my rock, in whom I take refuge, my shield and the horn of my salvation. He is my stronghold, my refuge and my savior—from violent men you save me.

Psalm 18:1-2

KJV—I will love thee, O Lord, my strength. The Lord is my rock, and my fortress, and my deliverer; my God, my strength, in whom I will trust; my buckler, and the horn of my salvation, and my high tower.

AMP—I love You fervently and devotedly, O Lord, my strength. The Lord is my rock, my fortress, and my deliverer; my God, my keen and firm strength in Whom I will trust and take refuge, my shield, and the horn of my salvation, my high tower.

Moffatt—O Eternal, my Strength, I will exalt thee. The Eternal is my crag, my stronghold, my deliverer, my God, my fortalice where I take shelter, my shield, my saving strength, my retreat.

NIV—I love you, O Lord, my strength. The Lord is my rock, my fortress and my deliverer; my God is my rock, in whom I take refuge. He is my shield and the horn of my salvation, my stronghold.

Psalm 31:1-3

NKJV—In You, O Lord, I put my trust.... Be my rock of refuge, A fortress of defense to save me. For You are my rock and my fortress.

Hidden in God

KJV—In thee, O Lord, do I put my trust.... Be thou my strong rock, for an house of defence to save me. For thou art my rock and my fortress.

Moffatt—With thee, O thou Eternal, I take shelter.... Be a rock of refuge for me, a hill-fort to protect me, for thou art my crag and castle.

NIV—In you, O Lord, I have taken refuge.... Be my rock of refuge, a strong fortress to save me. Since you are my rock and my fortress.

Psalm 46:1

KJV—God is our refuge and strength, a very present help in trouble.

AMP—God is our refuge and strength [mighty and impenetrable to temptation] a very present and well-proved help in trouble.

Moffatt—God is a shelter and stronghold for us, we shall find him very near.

NIV—God is our refuge and strength, an ever-present help in trouble.

Psalm 61:3

KJV—Thou hast been a shelter for me, and a strong tower from the enemy.

AMP—You have been a shelter and a refuge for me, a strong tower against the adversary.

Moffatt—O thou who art my refuge, a fortress against the foe.

NIV—You have been my refuge, a strong tower against the foe.

Psalm 62:6-8

KJV—He only is my rock and my salvation: he is my defence; I shall not be moved. In God is my salvation and my glory: the rock of my strength, and my refuge, is in God. Trust in him at all times; ye people, pour out your heart before him: God is a refuge for us.

AMP—He only is my rock and my salvation; He is my defense and my fortress; I shall not be moved. With God rests my salvation and my glory; my rock of unyielding strength and impenetrable hardness, and my refuge is in God! Trust, lean on, rely on and have confidence in Him at all times, you people; pour out your heart before Him. God is a refuge for us—a fortress and a high tower.

Moffatt—Rock, rescue, refuge, he is all to me, never shall I be overthrown. My safety and my honour rest on God; God is my strong rock and refuge. Always rely on him, my followers, pour out your prayers to him; God is a refuge for us.

NIV—He alone is my rock and my salvation; he is my fortress, I will not be shaken. My salvation and my honor depend on God; he is my mighty rock, my refuge. Trust in him at all times, O people; pour out your hearts to him, for God is our refuge.

Psalm 71:7

KJV—I am as a wonder unto many; but thou art my strong refuge.

NKJV—I have become as a wonder to many, But You are my strong refuge.

AMP—I am as a wonder and surprise to many, but You are my strong refuge.

NAS—I have become a marvel to many; For Thou art my strong refuge.

Psalm 91

KJV—He that dwelleth in the secret place of the most High shall abide under the shadow of the Almighty. I will say of the Lord, He is my refuge and my fortress: my God; in him will I trust. Surely he shall deliver thee from the snare of the fowler, and from the noisome pestilence. He shall cover thee with his feathers, and under his wings shalt thou trust: his truth shall be thy shield and buckler. Thou shalt not be afraid for the terror by night; nor for the arrow that flieth by day; Nor for the pestilence that walketh in darkness; nor for the destruction that wasteth at noonday. A thousand shall fall at thy side, and ten thousand at thy right hand; but it shall not come nigh thee. Only with thine eyes shalt thou behold and see the reward of the wicked. Because thou hast made the Lord, which is my refuge, even the most High, thy habitation; There shall no evil befall thee, neither shall any plague come nigh thy dwelling. For he shall give his angels charge over thee, to keep thee in all thy ways. They shall bear thee up in their hands, lest thou dash thy foot against a stone. Thou shalt tread upon the lion and adder: the young lion and the dragon shalt thou trample under feet. Because he hath set his love upon me, therefore will I deliver him: I will set him on high, because he hath known my name. He shall call upon me, and I will answer him: I will be with him in trouble; I will deliver him, and honour him. With long life will I satisfy him, and show him my salvation.

AMP—He who dwells in the secret place of the Most High shall remain stable and fixed under the shadow of the Almighty [Whose power no foe can withstand]. I will say of the Lord, He is my refuge and my fortress, my God, on Him I lean and rely, and in Him I (confidently) trust! For [then] He will deliver you from the snare of the fowler and from the deadly pestilence. [Then] He will cover you with His pinions, and under His wings shall you trust and find refuge; His truth and His faithfulness are a shield and a buckler. [Then] You shall not be afraid of the terror of the night, nor of the arrow [the evil plots and slanders of the wicked] that flies by day, Nor of the pestilence that stalks in darkness, nor of the destruction and sudden death that surprise and lay waste at noonday. [Then] A thousand may fall at your side, and ten thousand at your right hand, but it shall not come near you. Only a spectator shall you be [yourself inaccessible in the secret place of the Most High] as you witness the reward of the wicked. Because you have made the Lord your refuge, and the Most High your dwelling place, There shall no evil befall you, nor any plague or calamity come near your tent. For He will give His angels [especial] charge over you, to accompany and defend and preserve you in all your ways [of obedience and service]. They shall bear you up on their hands, lest you dash your foot against a stone. You shall tread upon the lion and adder, the young lion and the serpent shall you trample under foot. Because he has set his love upon Me, therefore will I deliver him; I will set him on high, because he knows and understands My name [has a personal knowledge of My mercy, love and kindness; trusts and relies on Me, knowing I will never forsake him, no, never]. He shall call upon Me, and I will answer him; I will be with him in trouble, I will deliver him and honor him. With long life will I satisfy him, and show him My salvation.

TLB—We live within the shadow of the Almighty, sheltered by the God who is above all gods. This I declare, that he alone

*Protection
Promises*

is my refuge, my place of safety; he is my God, and I am trusting him. For he rescues you from every trap, and protects you from the fatal plague. He will shield you with his wings! They will shelter you. His faithful promises are your armor. Now you don't need to be afraid of the dark any more, nor fear the dangers of the day; nor dread the plagues of darkness, nor disasters in the morning. Though a thousand fall at my side, though ten thousand are dying around me, the evil will not touch me. I will see how the wicked are punished but I will not share it. For Jehovah is my refuge! I choose the God above all gods to shelter me. How then can evil overtake me or any plague come near? For he orders his angels to protect you wherever you go. They will steady you with their hands to keep you from stumbling against the rocks on the trail. You can safely meet a lion or step on poisonous snakes, yes, even trample them beneath your feet! For the Lord says, "Because he loves me, I will rescue him; I will make him great because he trusts in my name. When he calls on me I will answer; I will be with him in trouble, and rescue him and honor him. I will satisfy him with a full life and give him my salvation."

Psalm 94:22

KJV—The Lord is my defence; and my God is the rock of my refuge.

AMP—The Lord has become my high tower and defense, and my God, the rock of my refuge.

Moffatt—The Eternal who is my protection, my God who is my strength, my safety.

NIV—The Lord has become my fortress, and my God the rock in whom I take refuge.

Isaiah 26:1-2

AMP—We have a strong city; the Lord sets up salvation as walls and bulwarks. Open the gates, that the [uncompromisingly] righteous nation which keeps her faith and her troth with God may enter in.

NKJV—We have a strong city; God will appoint salvation for walls and bulwarks. Open the gates, That the righteous nation which keeps the truth may enter in.

Moffatt—Ours is a strong, sure city, safe with walls and ramparts set by Him; open its gates for the upright, for folk who keep the faith.

NIV—We have a strong city; God makes salvation its walls and ramparts. Open the gates that the righteous nation may enter, the nation that keeps faith.

Your Way of Escape

Psalm 71:2

KJV—Deliver me in thy righteousness, and cause me to escape: incline thine ear unto me, and save me.

AMP—Deliver me in Your righteousness and cause me to escape; bow down Your ear to me and save me!

Moffatt—Rescue me, save me, as thou art faithful, turn thine ear to me and deliver me.

NIV—Rescue me and deliver me in your righteousness; turn your ear to me and save me.

Psalm 141:10

KJV—Let the wicked fall into their own nets, whilst that I withal escape.

AMP—Let the wicked fall together into their own nets, while I pass over them and escape.

Moffatt—Let the ungodly fall into their own net, while I pass on rejoicing!

NIV—Let the wicked fall into their own nets, while I pass by in safety.

Daniel 3:17

KJV—Our God whom we serve is able to deliver us from the burning fiery furnace, and he will deliver us out of thine hand.

NKJV—Our God whom we serve is able to deliver us from the burning fiery furnace, and He will deliver us from your hand.

Moffatt—There is a God able to save us, the God whom we serve, able to save us from the burning furnace and from your power.

NAS—Our God whom we serve is able to deliver us from the furnace of blazing fire; and He will deliver us out of your hand.

132

*Protection
Promises*

Chapter 7

Freedom
From Fear

*Forasmuch then as the children
are partakers of flesh and
blood, he also himself likewise
took part of the same;
that through death he might
destroy him that had the power
of death, that is, the devil;
And deliver them who through
fear of death were all their
lifetime subject to bondage.*

Hebrews 2:14-15

God hath not given us the spirit of fear;
but of power, and of love,
and of a sound mind.
2 Timothy 1:7

If people knew how death operates, they wouldn't be so afraid to live. Jesus said that the one who believes on Him will never see death. We've passed from that place where we will know any death.

Fear of death is an enemy to you. Fear of any kind is an enemy. Fear will keep you from walking in God's delivering power. That's because God responds to faith. He does what we believe for Him to do.

If we have fear of death, we're living in fear. As a result, we give God no faith to work with. He intervenes in this earth through faith. Faith is what causes the power of God to come upon your body and heal you of sickness and disease. If we believe His promises to secure our lives, He secures our lives. Faith in God is what causes His angels to go forth and to protect you in times of trouble or times of danger.

The thing God says repeatedly in His Word is, "Fear not." Your deliverance is in fearing not and instead believing God. Fear not. But have faith in God.

People ruin their lives over the fear of danger, when there is no danger for the person who is inside of God's covenant of salvation. The definition of the word *salvation* includes "deliverance, preservation, material and temporal deliverance from danger and apprehension, or the fear of danger."

Take on the attitude of the three young Israelite men who were told to bow to a foreign god or face a fiery furnace. They replied, "We serve God and we believe that He is able to deliver us out of your hand. But, if not, just get this straight, King, we're not going to bow to other gods." Notice that attitude. They had more fear of the Lord than they had fear of death.

Why fear when you know angels have been assigned to be ministers of God's covenant promises—including promises of protection? You can hire bodyguards, but they're not as good as the angels. When you go to bed at night, you ought to thank God for the angels that encamp around about you to deliver you. When you put your head down on the pillow at night, you don't have to be afraid somebody's going to break into your house. Use your faith and believe God, thanking Him for the ministry of angels on your behalf and that you have protection. That's part of your salvation. Enjoy the rest of being free from fear as a covenant child of God. It belongs to you.

Overcoming Terror

Matthew 10:28-31

KJV—Fear not them which kill the body, but are not able to kill the soul: but rather fear him which is able to destroy both soul and body in hell. Are not two sparrows sold for a farthing? and one of them shall not fall on the ground without your Father. But the very hairs of your head are all numbered. Fear ye not therefore, ye are of more value than many sparrows.

AMP—Do not be afraid of those who kill the body but cannot kill the soul, but rather be afraid of him who can destroy both soul and body in hell (Gehenna). Are not two little sparrows sold for a penny? And yet not one of them will fall to the ground without your Father's leave and notice. But even the very hairs of your head are all numbered. Fear not, then; you are of more value than many sparrows.

Weymouth—Do not fear those who kill the body, but cannot kill the soul; rather fear Him who is able to destroy both soul and body in Gehenna. Do not two sparrows sell for a half penny? Yet not one of them falls to the ground without your Father's leave. But as for you, the very hairs on your heads are all numbered. Away then with fear; you are more precious than a multitude of sparrows.

NIV—Do not be afraid of those who kill the body but cannot kill the soul. Rather, be afraid of the One who can destroy both soul and body in hell. Are not two sparrows sold for a penny? Yet not one of them will fall to the ground apart from the will of your Father. And even the very hairs of your head are all numbered. So don't be afraid; you are worth more than many sparrows.

Matthew 24:4-6

KJV—Jesus answered and said unto them, Take heed that no man deceive you. For many shall come in my name, saying, I am Christ; and shall deceive many. And ye shall hear of wars and rumours of wars: see that ye be not troubled: for all these things must come to pass, but the end is not yet.

AMP—Jesus answered them, Be careful that no one [misleads] you—deceiving you and leading you into error. For many will come in (on the strength of) My name—appropriating the name which belongs to Me—saying, I am the Messiah, the Christ; and they will lead many astray. And you will hear of wars and rumors of wars; see that you are not frightened or troubled, for this must take place, but the end is not yet.

Weymouth—"Take care that no one misleads you," answered Jesus; "for many will come assuming my name and saying, 'I am the Christ'; and they will mislead many.

And you are to hear of wars and rumors of wars. See that you be not alarmed, for such things must be; but the end is not yet."

NIV—Jesus answered: "Watch out that no one deceives you. For many will come in my name, claiming, 'I am the Christ,' and will deceive many. You will hear of wars and rumors of wars, but see to it that you are not alarmed. Such things must happen, but the end is still to come."

Mark 5:36

KJV—Be not afraid, only believe.

AMP—Do not be seized with alarm and have no fear, only keep on believing.

Weymouth—Do not be afraid: only have faith.

NIV—Don't be afraid; just believe.

John 14:23, 27

KJV—Jesus answered...Peace I leave with you, my peace I give unto you: not as the world giveth, give I unto you. Let not your heart be troubled, neither let it be afraid.

AMP—Jesus answered...Peace I leave with you; My [own] peace I now give and bequeath to you. Not as the world gives do I give to you. Do not let your heart be troubled, neither let it be afraid—stop allowing yourselves to be agitated and disturbed;

and do not permit yourselves to be fearful and intimidated and cowardly and unsettled.

Weymouth—Jesus [replied]...Peace I leave with you: my own peace I give to you. Not as the world gives do I give to you. Let not your hearts be troubled or dismayed.

NIV—Jesus replied...Peace I leave with you; my peace I give you. I do not give to you as the world gives. Do not let your hearts be troubled and do not be afraid.

Hebrews 2:14-15

KJV—Forasmuch then as the children are partakers of flesh and blood, he also himself likewise took part of the same; that through death he might destroy him that had the power of death, that is, the devil; And deliver them who through fear of death were all their lifetime subject to bondage.

AMP—Since, therefore, [these His] children share in flesh and blood—that is, in the physical nature of human beings—He [Himself] in a similar manner partook of the same [nature], that by [going through] death He might bring to nought and make of no effect him who had the power of death, that is, the devil; And also that He might deliver and completely set free all those who through the (haunting) fear of death were held in bondage throughout the whole course of their lives.

Weymouth—Since, then, the children referred to are all alike sharers in perishable human nature, He Himself also, in the same way, took on Him a share of it, in order that through death He might render powerless him who had authority over death, that is, the devil, and might set at liberty all those who through fear of death had been subject to lifelong slavery.

NIV—Since the children have flesh and blood, he too shared in their humanity so that by his death he might destroy him who holds the power of death—that is, the devil—and free those who all their lives were held in slavery by their fear of death.

Overcoming the Spirit of Fear

Deuteronomy 20:1, 3-4

KJV—When thou goest out to battle against thine enemies, and seest horses, and chariots, and a people more than thou, be not afraid of them: for the Lord thy God is with thee, which brought thee up out of the land of Egypt…. Let not your hearts faint, fear not, and do not tremble, neither be ye terrified because of them; For the Lord your God is he that goeth with you, to fight for you against your enemies, to save you.

AMP—When you go forth to battle against your enemies, and see horses and chariots and an army greater than your own, do not be afraid of them; for the Lord your God, Who brought you out of the land of Egypt, is with you…. Let not your [minds and] hearts faint; fear not, and do not tremble, or be terrified (and in dread) because of them. For the Lord your God is He Who goes with you, to fight for you against your enemies, to save you.

Moffatt—When you set out to make war upon your enemies, and see war-horses and chariots and an army larger than yourselves, you must not be afraid of them, for the Eternal your God who brought you out of the land of Egypt is on your side…. Never lose heart, fear not, tremble not, be not afraid of them, for the Eternal your God goes with you, to fight for you against your enemies and to give you the victory.

NIV—When you go to war against your enemies and see horses and chariots and an army greater than yours, do not be afraid of them, because the Lord your God, who brought you up out of Egypt, will be with you…. Do not be fainthearted or afraid; do not be terrified or give way to panic before them. For the Lord your God is the one who goes with you to fight for you against your enemies to give you victory.

Psalm 91:5-6

KJV—Thou shalt not be afraid for the terror by night; nor for the arrow that flieth by day; Nor for the pestilence that walketh in darkness; nor for the destruction that wasteth at noonday.

AMP—You shall not be afraid of the terror of the night, nor of the arrow [the evil plots and slanders of the wicked] that flies by day, Nor of the pestilence that stalks in darkness, nor of the destruction and sudden death that surprise and lay waste at noonday.

Moffatt—You need not fear the terrors of the night, nor arrows flying in the day; you need not fear plague stalking in the dark, nor sudden death at noon.

NIV—You will not fear the terror of night, nor the arrow that flies by day, nor the pestilence that stalks in the darkness, nor the plague that destroys at midday.

Isaiah 35:3-4

KJV—Strengthen ye the weak hands, and confirm the feeble knees. Say to them that are of a fearful heart, Be strong, fear not: behold, your God will come with vengeance, even God with a recompence; he will come and save you.

AMP—Strengthen the weak hands, and make firm the feeble and tottering knees. Say to those who are of a fearful and hasty heart, Be strong, fear not! Behold, your God will come with vengeance, with the recompense of God; He will come and save you.

Moffatt—Put heart into the listless, and brace all weak-kneed souls, tell men with fluttering hearts, "Have courage, never fear; here comes your God, he will avenge his folk, here comes God's retribution, he comes himself to save you!"

NIV—Strengthen the feeble hands, steady the knees that give way; say to those with fearful hearts, "Be strong, do not fear; your God will come, he will come with vengeance; with divine retribution he will come to save you."

2 Timothy 1:7

KJV—God hath not given us the spirit of fear; but of power, and of love, and of a sound mind.

AMP—God did not give us a spirit of timidity—of cowardice, of craven and cringing and fawning fear—but [He has given us a spirit] of power and of love and of calm and well-balanced mind and discipline and self-control.

Weymouth—The spirit which God has given us is not a spirit of cowardice, but one of power and of love and of self-discipline.

NIV—God did not give us a spirit of timidity, but a spirit of power, of love and of self-discipline.

Overcoming Fear of Abandonment

Deuteronomy 31:6, 8

KJV—Be strong and of a good courage, fear not, nor be afraid of them: for the Lord thy God, he it is that doth go with thee; he will not fail thee, nor forsake thee.... The Lord, he it is that doth go before thee; he will be with thee, he will not fail thee, neither forsake thee: fear not, neither be dismayed.

AMP—Be strong, courageous and firm, fear not, nor be in terror before them; for it is the Lord your God Who goes with you; He will not fail you or forsake you.... It is the Lord Who goes before you; He will [march] with you; He will not fail you or let you go, or forsake you; [let there be no cowardice or flinching, but] fear not, neither become broken [in spirit] (depressed, dismayed and unnerved with alarm).

Moffatt—Be strong, be brave, fear not, be not terrified of them; for it is the Eternal your God who goes with you, he will never fail you nor forsake you.... It is the Eternal who leads you, he will be with you, he will never fail you nor forsake you: fear not, neither be dismayed.

NIV—Be strong and courageous. Do not be afraid or terrified because of them, for the Lord your God goes with you; he will never leave you nor forsake you.... The Lord

144

Protection
Promises

himself goes before you and will be with you; he will never leave you nor forsake you. Do not be afraid; do not be discouraged.

Joshua 1:1, 5

KJV—The Lord spake unto Joshua...saying...As I was with Moses, so I will be with thee: I will not fail thee, nor forsake thee.

AMP—The Lord said to Joshua...As I was with Moses, so I will be with you; I will not fail you or forsake you.

Moffatt—The Eternal said to Joshua..."As I was with Moses, so I will be with you; I will never fail you nor forsake you."

NIV—The Lord said to Joshua..."As I was with Moses, so I will be with you; I will never leave you nor forsake you."

Joshua 1:9

KJV—Be strong and of a good courage; be not afraid, neither be thou dismayed: for the Lord thy God is with thee whithersoever thou goest.

AMP—Be strong, vigorous and very courageous; be not afraid, neither be dismayed; for the Lord your God is with you wherever you go.

Moffatt—Be firm and brave, never be daunted or dismayed, for the Eternal your God is with you wherever you go.

NIV—Be strong and courageous. Do not be terrified; do not be discouraged, for the Lord your God will be with you wherever you go.

Matthew 1:23

KJV—A virgin shall be with child, and shall bring forth a son, and they shall call his name Emmanuel, which being interpreted is, God with us.

AMP—The virgin shall become pregnant and give birth to a Son, and they shall call His name Emmanuel, which when translated means, God with us.

Weymouth—The maiden will be with child and will give birth to a son, And they will give him the name Immanuel—a word which signifies "God with us."

NIV—The virgin will be with child and will give birth to a son, and they will call him Immanuel—which means, "God with us."

Matthew 28:18, 20

KJV—And Jesus came and spake unto them, saying...Lo, I am with you alway, even unto the end of the world.

AMP—Jesus approached and breaking the silence said to them...Lo, I am with you all the days,—perpetually, uniformly and on every occasion—to the [very] close and consummation of the age.

Weymouth—Jesus, however, came near and said to them... Remember, I am with you always, day by day, until the close of the age.

NIV—Then Jesus came to them and said... "Surely I am with you always, to the very end of the age."

Hebrews 13:5

AMP—He (God) Himself has said, I will not in any way fail you nor give you up nor leave you without support. [I will] not, [I will] not, [I will] not in any degree leave you helpless, nor forsake nor let [you] down, [relax my hold on you].—Assuredly not!

KJV—He hath said, I will never leave thee, nor forsake thee.

NIV—God has said, "Never will I leave you; never will I forsake you."

Moffatt—He has said, Never will I fail you. Never will I forsake you.

Freedom From Fear

Overcoming Fear of Man

Numbers 14:6-7, 9

KJV—Joshua the son of Nun, and Caleb the son of Jephunneh...spake unto all the company of the children of Israel, saying... Rebel not ye against the Lord, neither fear ye the people of the land; for they are bread for us: their defence is departed from them, and the Lord is with us: fear them not.

AMP—Joshua son of Nun and Caleb son of Jephunneh...said to all the company of Israelites...Do not rebel against the Lord, neither fear the people of the land; for they are bread for us; their defense and the shadow [of protection] is removed from over them, but the Lord is with us; fear them not.

Moffatt—Joshua the son of Nun and Caleb the son of Jephunneh...told all the assembly of the Israelites..."Rebel not against the Eternal. And have no fear of the natives—we shall eat them up; their protection has failed, and the Eternal is with us; fear them not."

NIV—Joshua son of Nun and Caleb son of Jephunneh...said to the entire Israelite assembly..."Do not rebel against the Lord. And do not be afraid of the people of the land, because we will swallow them up. Their protection is gone, but the Lord is with us. Do not be afraid of them."

Psalm 27:1

KJV—The Lord is my light and my salvation; whom shall I fear? the Lord is the strength of my life; of whom shall I be afraid?

TLB—The Lord is my light and my salvation; whom shall I fear?

Psalm 56:3-4

NKJV—Whenever I am afraid, I will trust in You. In God (I will praise His word), In God I have put my trust; I will not fear. What can flesh do to me?

AMP—What time I am afraid, I will have confidence and put my trust and reliance on You. By [the help of] God I will praise His Word; on God I lean, rely, and confidently put my trust; I will not fear; what can man who is flesh do to me?

Moffatt—The day I am afraid, I put my trust in thee. By God's help I shall maintain my cause; in God I trust without a fear: what can man do to me?

NIV—When I am afraid, I will trust in you. In God, whose word I praise, in God I trust; I will not be afraid. What can mortal man do to me?

Psalm 118:6

KJV—The Lord is on my side; I will not fear: what can man do unto me?

AMP—The Lord is on my side; I will not fear. What can man do to me?

Moffatt—The Eternal is upon my side; I have no fear. What can man do to me?

NIV—The Lord is with me; I will not be afraid. What can man do to me?

Isaiah 41:10-14

KJV—Fear thou not; for I am with thee: be not dismayed; for I am thy God: I will strengthen thee; yea, I will help thee; yea, I will uphold thee with the right hand of my righteousness. Behold, all they that were incensed against thee shall be ashamed and confounded: they shall be as nothing; and they that strive with thee shall perish. Thou shalt seek them, and shalt not find them, even them that contended with thee: they that war against thee shall be as nothing, and as a thing of nought. For I the Lord thy God will hold thy right hand, saying unto thee, Fear not; I will help thee. Fear not... saith the Lord, and thy redeemer, the Holy One of Israel.

AMP—Fear not; [there is nothing to fear] for I am with you; do not look around you in terror and be dismayed, for I am your God. I will strengthen and harden you [to difficulties]; yes, I will help you; yes, I will hold you up and retain you with My victorious right hand of rightness and justice. Behold, all they who are enraged and inflamed against you shall be put to shame and confounded; they who strive against you shall be as nothing and shall perish. You shall seek those who contend with you, and shall not find them; they who war against you shall be as nothing, as nothing at all. For I, the Lord your God, hold your right hand; I,

Who say to you, Fear not, I will help you! Fear not,...says the Lord; your Redeemer is the Holy One of Israel.

Moffatt—Fear not, for I am with you, I am your God, be not dismayed; I will strengthen, I will support you, I will uphold you with my trusty hand. All who are enraged at you shall be defeated and confounded, those who quarrel with you shall vanish into nothing; you will not find them when you look for them, those men who strove with you: they shall turn to a mere nothing, those who war against you. For I the Eternal your God hold you by the hand, whispering, "Fear not, I will help you." Fear not...your champion is the Majestic One of Israel—it is the Eternal's promise.

NIV—"So do not fear, for I am with you; do not be dismayed, for I am your God. I will strengthen you and help you; I will uphold you with my righteous right hand. All who rage against you will surely be ashamed and disgraced; those who oppose you will be as nothing and perish. Though you search for your enemies, you will not find them. Those who wage war against you will be as nothing at all. For I am the Lord, your God, who takes hold of your right hand and says to you, Do not fear; I will help you. Do not be afraid..." declares the Lord, your Redeemer, the Holy One of Israel.

Isaiah 51:12

KJV—I...am he that comforteth you: who art thou, that thou shouldest be afraid of a man that shall die, and of the son of man which shall be made as grass.

AMP—I...am He Who comforts you. Who are you, that you should be afraid of man who shall die, and of a son of man who shall be made [as destructible] as grass.

Moffatt—I am he who comforts you; how can you ever be afraid of mortal men, of men on earth who like the grass shall fade?

NIV—I...am he who comforts you. Who are you that you fear mortal men, the sons of men, who are but grass.

Jeremiah 1:8

KJV—Be not afraid of their faces: for I am with thee to deliver thee, saith the Lord.

AMP—Be not afraid of them [their faces], for I am with you to deliver you, says the Lord.

Moffatt—"Be not afraid at the sight of them, for I am with you to succour you." The Eternal said it.

NIV—"Do not be afraid of them, for I am with you and will rescue you," declares the Lord.

Jeremiah 15:20-21

KJV—They shall fight against thee, but they shall not prevail against thee: for I am with thee to save thee and to deliver thee, saith the Lord. And I will deliver thee out of the hand of the wicked, and I will redeem thee out of the hand of the terrible.

AMP—They will fight against you, but they shall not prevail over you; for I am with you to save and deliver you, says the Lord. And I will deliver you out of the hand of the wicked, and I will redeem you out of the palm of the terrible and ruthless tyrants.

Moffatt—"They shall attack you but not master you, for I am with you to succour you; I will deliver you from evil men, and free you from the clutches of the cruel."

NIV—"They will fight against you but will not overcome you, for I am with you to rescue and save you," declares the Lord. "I will save you from the hands of the wicked and redeem you from the grasp of the cruel."

Ezekiel 2:6

KJV—Son of man, be not afraid of them, neither be afraid of their words, though briers and thorns be with thee, and thou dost dwell among scorpions: be not afraid of their words, nor be dismayed at their looks.

AMP—Son of man, be not afraid of them, neither be afraid of their words; though briers and thorns are all around you and you dwell and sit among scorpions, be not afraid of their words, nor be dismayed at their looks.

Moffatt—Son of man, fear them not, fear not what they say, although they cut and wound you, these scorpions round you with their sting—fear not what they say, dread not their scowls.

NIV—Son of man, do not be afraid of them or their words. Do not be afraid, though briers and thorns are all around you and you live among scorpions. Do not be afraid of what they say or terrified by them.

Acts 18:9-10

KJV—Then spake the Lord to Paul in the night by a vision, Be not afraid, but speak, and hold not thy peace: For I am with thee, and no man shall set on thee to hurt thee.

AMP—One night the Lord said to Paul in a vision, Have no fear, but speak and do not keep silent; For I am with you, and no man shall assault you to harm you.

Weymouth—In a vision by night, the Lord said to Paul, "Dismiss your fears: go on speaking, and do not be silent. I am with you, and no one shall attack you to injure you."

NIV—One night the Lord spoke to Paul in a vision: "Do not be afraid; keep on speaking, do not be silent. For I am with you, and no one is going to attack and harm you."

Philippians 1:27-28

NKJV—Let your conduct be worthy of the gospel of Christ, so that whether I come and see you or am absent, I may hear of your affairs, that you stand fast in one spirit, with one mind striving together for the faith of the gospel, and not in any way terrified by your adversaries, which is to them a proof of perdition, but to you of salvation, and that from God.

AMP—Conduct yourselves that your manner of life will be worthy of the good news (the Gospel) of Christ, so that whether I [do] come and see you or am absent, I may hear this of you: that you are standing firm in united spirit and purpose, striving side by side and contending with a single mind for the faith of the glad tidings (the Gospel). And do not [for a moment] be frightened or intimidated in anything by your opponents and adversaries, for such [constancy and fearlessness] will be a clear sign (proof and seal) to them of [their impending] destruction; but [a sure token and evidence] of your deliverance and salvation, and that from God.

Weymouth—Let the lives you live be worthy of the gospel of the Christ, in order that, whether I come and see you or, being absent, only hear of you, I may know that you are standing fast in one spirit and with one mind, fighting shoulder to shoulder for the faith of the gospel. Never for a moment quail [draw back in fear] before your antagonists. Your fearlessness will be to them a sure token of impending destruction, but to you it will be a sure token of your salvation—a token coming from God.

NIV—Conduct yourselves in a manner worthy of the gospel of Christ. Then, whether I come and see you or only hear about you in my absence, I will know that you stand firm in one spirit, contending as one man for the faith of the gospel without being frightened in any way by those who oppose you. This is a sign to them that they will be destroyed, but that you will be saved—and that by God.

Overcoming Evil Reports

Psalm 3:6

KJV—I will not be afraid of ten thousands of people, that have set themselves against me round about.

AMP—I will not be afraid of ten thousands of people, who have set themselves against me round about.

Moffatt—I fear not thousands of the foe ranged all around me.

NIV—I will not fear the tens of thousands drawn up against me on every side.

Psalm 27:3

KJV—Though an host should encamp against me, my heart shall not fear: though war should rise against me, in this will I be confident.

AMP—Though a host encamp against me, my heart shall not fear; though war arise against me, (even then) in this will I be confident.

Moffatt—Even though an army were arrayed against me, my heart would have no fear; though war were waged on me, still would I be confident.

NIV—Though an army besiege me, my heart will not fear; though war break out against me, even then will I be confident.

Psalm 46:2-3

NKJV—We will not fear, Even though the earth be removed, And though the mountains be carried into the midst of the sea; Though its waters roar and be troubled, Though the mountains shake with its swelling.

AMP—We will not fear, though the earth should change, and though the mountains be shaken into the midst of the seas; Though its waters roar and foam, though the mountains tremble at its swelling and tumult.

Moffatt—We never fear, though earth be overset, though hills sink deep in the sea. Let billows roar and foam, let mountains shake under the storm.

*Freedom
From Fear*

NIV—We will not fear, though the earth give way and the mountains fall into the heart of the sea, though its waters roar and foam and the mountains quake with their surging.

Psalm 91:3-6

KJV—Surely he shall deliver thee from the snare of the fowler, and from the noisome pestilence. He shall cover thee with his feathers, and under his wings shalt thou trust: his truth shall be thy shield and buckler. Thou shalt not be afraid for the terror by night; nor for the arrow that flieth by day; Nor for the pestilence that walketh in darkness; nor for the destruction that wasteth at noonday.

AMP—For [then] He will deliver you from the snare of the fowler and from the deadly pestilence. [Then] He will cover you with His pinions, and under His wings shall you trust and find refuge; His truth and His faithfulness are a shield and a buckler. [Then] You shall not be afraid of the terror of the night, nor of the arrow [the evil plots and slanders of the wicked] that flies by day, Nor of the pestilence that stalks in darkness, nor of the destruction and sudden death that surprise and lay waste at noonday.

TLB—For he rescues you from every trap, and protects you from the fatal plague. He will shield you with his wings! They will

Protection
Promises

shelter you. His faithful promises are your armor. Now you don't need to be afraid of the dark any more, nor fear the dangers of the day; nor dread the plagues of darkness, nor disasters in the morning.

Psalm 112:1, 7-8

KJV—Blessed is the man that feareth the Lord, that delighteth greatly in his commandments.... He shall not be afraid of evil tidings: his heart is fixed, trusting in the Lord. His heart is established, he shall not be afraid.

AMP—Blessed—happy, fortunate [to be envied]—is the man who fears (reveres and worships) the Lord, who delights greatly in His commandments.... He shall not be afraid of evil tidings; his heart is firmly fixed, trusting (leaning on and being confident) in the Lord. His heart is established and steady, he will not be afraid.

Moffatt—Happy the man who reverences the Eternal, who finds rich joy in his commands.... He has no fear of evil tidings, he trusts the Eternal with a steady heart; his heart is firm and fearless.

NIV—Blessed is the man who fears the Lord, who finds great delight in his commands.... He will have no fear of bad news; his heart is steadfast, trusting in the Lord. His heart is secure, he will have no fear.

Angels—Agents of Protection

Genesis 24:40

KJV—He [Abraham] said unto me [his servant], The Lord, before whom I walk, will send his angel with thee, and prosper thy way.

AMP—And he [Abraham] said to me [his servant], The Lord, in Whose presence I walk (habitually), will send His Angel with you and prosper your way.

Moffatt—He [Abraham] answered [his servant], "The Eternal, of whose presence I am ever mindful, will send his angel along with you and make your journey a success."

NIV—He [Abraham] replied [to his servant], "The Lord, before whom I have walked, will send his angel with you and make your journey a success."

Exodus 23:20-23

KJV—Behold, I send an Angel before thee, to keep thee in the way, and to bring thee into the place which I have prepared. Beware of him, and obey his voice, provoke him not; for he will not pardon your transgressions: for my name is in him. But if thou shalt indeed obey his voice, and do all that I speak; then I will be an enemy unto thine enemies, and an adversary unto thine adversaries. For mine Angel shall go before thee.

AMP—Behold, I send an Angel before you to keep and guard you on the way and to bring you to the place I have prepared. Give heed to Him, listen to and obey His voice; be not rebellious before Him or provoke Him, for He will not pardon your transgression; for My name is in Him. But if you will indeed listen to and obey His voice and all that I speak, then I will be an enemy to your enemies and an adversary to your adversaries. When My Angel goes before you.

NIV—See, I am sending an angel ahead of you to guard you along the way and to bring you to the place I have prepared. Pay attention to him and listen to what he says. Do not rebel against him; he will not forgive your rebellion, since my Name is in him. If you listen carefully to what he says and do all that I say, I will be an enemy to your enemies and will oppose those who oppose you. My angel will go ahead of you.

NAS—Behold, I am going to send an angel before you to guard you along the way, and to bring you into the place which I have prepared. Be on your guard before him and obey his voice; do not be rebellious toward him, for he will not pardon your transgression, since My name is in him. But if you will truly obey his voice and do all that I say, then I will be an enemy to your enemies and an adversary to your adversaries. For My angel will go before you.

KJV—[Elisha] answered, Fear not: for they that be with us are more than they that be with them. And Elisha prayed, and said, Lord, I pray thee, open his eyes, that he may see. And the Lord opened the eyes of the young man; and he saw: and, behold, the mountain was full of horses and chariots of fire round about Elisha.

AMP—Elisha answered, Fear not; for those with us are more than those with them. Then Elisha prayed, Lord, I pray You, open his eyes that he may see. And the Lord opened the young man's eyes, and he saw; and behold, the mountain was full of horses and chariots of fire round about Elisha.

Moffatt—"Fear not," [Elisha] answered; "those on our side are more than those on their side." Then Elisha prayed, "O Eternal, open his eyes, that he may see." The Eternal did open the young man's eyes; and what he saw was the hill covered with horses and chariots of fire around Elisha!

NIV—"Don't be afraid," the prophet answered, "Those who are with us are more than those who are with them." And Elisha prayed, "O Lord, open his eyes so he may see." Then the Lord opened the servant's eyes, and he looked and saw the hills full of horses and chariots of fire all around Elisha.

Psalm 103:20-22

KJV—Bless the Lord, ye his angels, that excel in strength, that do his commandments, hearkening unto the voice of his word. Bless ye the Lord, all ye his hosts; ye ministers of his, that do his pleasure. Bless the Lord, all his works in all places of his dominion: bless the Lord, O my soul.

AMP—Bless—affectionately, gratefully praise—the Lord, you His angels, you mighty ones who do His commandments, hearkening to the voice of His word. Bless—affectionately, gratefully praise—the Lord, all you His hosts, you ministers of His who do His pleasure. Bless the Lord, all His works in all places of His dominion; bless—affectionately, gratefully praise—the Lord, O my soul!

Moffatt—Bless the Eternal, O his angels, ye strong spirits who obey his word! Bless the Eternal, all his hosts, ye servants who carry out his will! Bless the Eternal, all his works in every sphere of his dominion!

NIV—Praise the Lord, you his angels, you mighty ones who do his bidding, who obey his word. Praise the Lord, all his heavenly hosts, you his servants who do his will. Praise the Lord, all his works everywhere in his dominion. Praise the Lord, O my soul.

Acts 5:17-20

KJV—Then the high priest rose up, and all they that were with him, (which is the sect of the Sadducees,) and were filled with indignation, And laid their hands on the apostles, and put them in the common prison. But the angel of the Lord by night opened the prison doors, and brought them forth, and said, Go, stand and speak in the temple to the people all the words of this life.

Acts 12:5-11

KJV—Peter therefore was kept in prison: but prayer was made without ceasing of the church unto God for him. And when Herod would have brought him forth, the same night Peter was sleeping between two soldiers, bound with two chains: and the keepers before the door kept the prison. And, behold, the angel of the Lord came upon him, and a light shined in the prison: and he smote Peter on the side, and raised him up, saying, Arise up quickly. And his chains fell off from his hands. And the angel said unto him, Gird thyself, and bind on thy sandals. And so he did. And he saith unto him, Cast thy garment about thee, and follow me. And he went out, and followed him; and wist not that it was true which was done by the angel; but thought he saw a vision. When they were past the first and the second ward, they came unto the iron gate that leadeth unto the city; which opened to them of his own accord: and they went out, and passed on through one street; and forthwith the angel departed from him. And when Peter was come to himself, he said, Now I know of a surety, that the Lord hath sent his angel, and hath delivered me out of the hand of Herod, and from all the expectation of the people of the Jews.

Acts 27:23-25

KJV—There stood by me [Paul] this night the angel of God, whose I am, and whom I serve, Saying, Fear not.... [So,] sirs, be of good cheer: for I believe God, that it shall be even as it was told me.

AMP—This [very] night there stood by my [Paul's] side an angel of the God to Whom I belong and Whom I serve and worship, And he said, Do not be frightened.... So keep up your courage, men, for I have faith—complete confidence—in God that it will be exactly as it was told me.

Weymouth—There stood by my [Paul's] side, last night, an angel of the God to whom I belong, and whom also I worship, and he said, "Dismiss all fear...." Therefore, Sirs, take courage; for I believe God, and am convinced that things will happen exactly as I have been told.

NIV—Last night an angel of the God whose I am and whom I serve stood beside me [Paul] and said, "Do not be afraid...." So keep up your courage, men, for I have faith in God that it will happen just as he told me.

Hebrews 1:13-14

KJV—But to which of the angels said he at any time, Sit on my right hand, until I make thine enemies thy footstool? Are they not all ministering spirits, sent forth to minister for them who shall be heirs of salvation?

AMP—Besides, to which of the angels has He ever said, Sit at My right hand—associated with Me in My royal dignity—till I make your enemies a stool for your feet? Are not the angels all (servants) ministering spirits, sent out in the service [of God for the assistance] of those who are to inherit salvation?

Moffatt—To what angel did he ever say, "Sit at my right hand, till I make your enemies a foot-stool for your feet"? Are not all angels merely spirits in the divine service, commissioned for the benefit of those who are to inherit salvation?

NIV—To which of the angels did God ever say, "Sit at my right hand until I make your enemies a footstool for your feet"? Are not all angels ministering spirits sent to serve those who will inherit salvation?

Chapter 8

Safety for Your Family

Know therefore that the Lord your God is God; he is the faithful God, keeping his covenant of love to a thousand generations of those who love him and keep his commands.
Deuteronomy 7:9, NIV

Whoso shall receive one such little child in my name receiveth me. But whoso shall offend one of these little ones which believe in me, it were better for him that a millstone were hanged about his neck, and that he were drowned in the depth of the sea.

Matthew 18:5-6

God is a Father. By His very nature, He wants to protect and nurture His children. The Father's tender heart is revealed in many scriptures. For example, Luke 13:34 says, "*How often would I have gathered thy children together, as a hen doth gather her brood under her wings.*" And Psalm 91:4 says, "*He shall cover thee with his feathers, and under his wings shalt thou trust.*"

Because of covenant, God saved Noah and his family. Because of covenant, He began a heritage of faith through Abraham, and He delivered Moses and the Israelites.

God keeps His covenant to a thousand generations. Now that's a lot of family! What that means to God is not only did your step of faith change your future, but it also changed the future of your children and grandchildren.

If your family members are in unsafe circumstances, you can confess Ezekiel 34:12,

"I *seek out my sheep, and will deliver them out of all places...*" and claim their deliverance.

If your children need to be gathered in, you can pray Isaiah 43:5, "I *will bring your children from the east...*" (NIV), and call them in by faith.

If you feel alone, you can stand on Psalm 68:5, for God is "*a father to the fatherless, a defender of widows*" (NIV), and know that God cares for you.

God wants to bless and protect you and your family.

Genesis 22:17-18

NKJV—Blessing I will bless you, and multiplying I will multiply your descendants as the stars of the heaven and as the sand which is on the seashore; and your descendants shall possess the gate of their enemies. In your seed all the nations of the earth shall be blessed, because you have obeyed My voice.

AMP—In blessing I will bless you, and in multiplying I will multiply your descendants as the stars of the heavens and as the sand on the seashore. And your Seed (Heir) shall possess the gate of His enemies; And in your Seed [Christ] shall all the nations of the earth be blessed and [by Him] bless themselves, because you have heard and obeyed My voice.

Moffatt—I will indeed bless you, I will indeed make your descendants as numerous as the stars in the sky and the sand on the sea-shore; your descendants shall conquer the seats of their foes, and all nations on earth shall seek bliss like theirs—and all because you have obeyed my word.

NIV—I will surely bless you and make your descendants as numerous as the stars in the sky and as the sand on the seashore. Your descendants will take possession of the cities of their enemies, and through your offspring all nations on earth will be blessed, because you have obeyed me.

Deuteronomy 4:40

KJV—Thou shalt keep therefore his statutes, and his commandments, which I command thee this day, that it may go well with thee, and with thy children after thee, and that thou mayest prolong thy days upon the earth, which the Lord thy God giveth thee, for ever.

AMP—You shall keep His statutes and His commandments, which I command you this day, that it may go well with you and your children after you, and that you may prolong your days in the land which the Lord your God gives you for ever.

Moffatt—You must obey his rules and orders which I command you this day, that all may go well with you and with your children after you, and that you may live long on the land which the Eternal your God assigns you.

NIV—Keep his decrees and commands, which I am giving you today, so that it may go well with you and your children after you and that you may live long in the land the Lord your God gives you for all time.

Deuteronomy 7:9

KJV—Know therefore that the Lord thy God, he is God, the faithful God, which keepeth covenant and mercy with them that love him and keep his commandments to a thousand generations.

AMP—Know, recognize and understand therefore that the Lord your God, He is God, the faithful God, Who keeps covenant and steadfast love and mercy with those who love Him and keep His commandments, to a thousand generations.

Moffatt—Understand, then, that the Eternal your God is God indeed, a faithful God who carries out his compact of kindness to those who love him and carry out his orders, for a thousand generations.

NIV—Know therefore that the Lord your God is God; he is the faithful God, keeping his covenant of love to a thousand generations of those who love him and keep his commands.

Deuteronomy 12:28

KJV—Observe and hear all these words which I command thee, that it may go well with thee, and with thy children after thee for ever, when thou doest that which is good and right in the sight of the Lord thy God.

AMP—Be watchful and obey all these words which I command you, that it may go well with you and with your children after you for ever, when you do what is good and right in the sight of the Lord your God.

Moffatt—Listen carefully to all these orders of mine, that things may go well with you and with your children after you for all time, as you do what is good and right in the eyes of the Eternal your God.

NIV—Be careful to obey all these regulations I am giving you, so that it may always go well with you and your children after you, because you will be doing what is good and right in the eyes of the Lord your God.

Deuteronomy 30:19-20

KJV—I call heaven and earth to record this day against you, that I have set before you life and death, blessing and cursing: therefore choose life, that both thou and thy seed may live: That thou mayest love the Lord thy God, and that thou mayest obey his voice, and that thou mayest cleave unto him: for he is thy life, and the length of thy days: that thou mayest dwell in the land which the Lord sware unto thy fathers, to Abraham, to Isaac, and to Jacob, to give them.

Psalm 37:25

NKJV—I have been young, and now am old; Yet I have not seen the righteous forsaken, Nor his descendants begging bread.

AMP—I have been young and now am old, yet have I not seen the [uncompromisingly] righteous forsaken or his seed begging bread.

NIV—I was young and now I am old, yet I have never seen the righteous forsaken or their children begging bread.

NAS—I have been young, and now I am old; Yet I have not seen the righteous forsaken, Or his descendants begging bread.

Psalm 103:13, 17-18

KJV—Like as a father pitieth his children, so the Lord pitieth them that fear him... The mercy of the Lord is from everlasting to everlasting upon them that fear him, and his righteousness unto children's children; To such as keep his covenant, and to those that remember his commandments to do them.

AMP—As a father loves and pities his children, so the Lord loves and pities those who fear Him—with reverence, worship and awe... The mercy and loving-kindness of the

Lord are from everlasting to everlasting upon those who reverently and worshipfully fear Him, and His righteousness is to children's children, To such as keep His covenant—hearing, receiving, loving and obeying it; and to those who [earnestly] remember His commandments to do them [imprinting them on their hearts].

Moffatt—As a father pities his children, so the Eternal pities his worshippers.... The Eternal's love is everlasting, his loyalty goes on to children's children, when they obey his compact and remember to do his bidding.

NIV—As a father has compassion on his children, so the Lord has compassion on those who fear him... From everlasting to everlasting the Lord's love is with those who fear him, and his righteousness with their children's children—with those who keep his covenant and remember to obey his precepts.

Protection
Promises

Proverbs 4:3-4

KJV—For I was my father's son, tender and only beloved in the sight of my mother. He taught me also, and said unto me, Let thine heart retain my words: keep my commandments, and live.

AMP—When I [Solomon] was a son with my father [David], tender and the only one in the sight of my mother [Bathsheba], He taught me, and said to me, Let your heart hold fast my words; keep my commandments and live.

Moffatt—When I was a son with my father, a little one, loved by my mother, he taught me and told me this: "Keep in mind what I say, do what I bid you, and you shall live, swerve not from my orders."

NIV—When I was a boy in my father's house, still tender, and an only child of my mother, he taught me and said, "Lay hold of my words with all your heart; keep my commands and you will live."

Proverbs 14:26

NIV—He who fears the Lord has a secure fortress, and for his children it will be a refuge.

NKJV—In the fear of the Lord there is strong confidence, And His children will have a place of refuge.

AMP—In the reverent and worshipful fear of the Lord is strong confidence, and His children shall always have a place of refuge.

Moffatt—He who reverences the Eternal has strong ground for confidence; his very children win security.

Isaiah 43:4-6

KJV—Since thou wast precious in my sight, thou hast been honourable, and I have loved thee...Fear not: for I am with thee: I will bring thy seed from the east, and gather thee from the west...bring my sons from far, and my daughters from the ends of the earth.

AMP—You are precious in My sight, and honored, and I love you...Fear not, for I am with you; I will bring your offspring from the east [where they are dispersed], and gather you from the west...bring My sons from afar and My daughters from the ends of the earth.

Moffatt—So precious are you to me, so honoured, so beloved...From the far east will I bring your offspring, and from the far west I will gather you...bringing my sons from afar, and my daughters from the end of the earth.

NIV—Since you are precious and honored in my sight, and because I love you...Do not be afraid, for I am with you; I will bring your children from the east and gather you from the west...Bring my sons from afar and my daughters from the ends of the earth.

Isaiah 49:25

NKJV—But thus says the Lord: "Even the captives of the mighty shall be taken away, And the prey of the terrible be delivered; For I will contend with him who contends with you, And I will save your children.

AMP—For thus says the Lord, Even the captives of the mighty shall be taken away, and the prey of the terrible shall be delivered; for I will contend with him who contends with you, and I will give safety to your children and ease them.

NIV—But this is what the Lord says: "Yes, captives will be taken from warriors, and plunder retrieved from the fierce; I will contend with those who contend with you, and your children I will save.

NAS—Surely, thus says the Lord, "Even the captives of the mighty man will be taken away, And the prey of the tyrant will be rescued; For I will contend with the one who contends with you, And I will save your sons."

Matthew 18:1-6

KJV—At the same time came the disciples unto Jesus, saying, Who is the greatest in the kingdom of heaven?

And Jesus called a little child unto him, and set him in the midst of them, And said, Verily I say unto you, Except ye be converted, and become as little children, ye shall not enter into the kingdom of heaven. Whosoever therefore shall humble himself as this little child, the same is greatest in the kingdom of heaven.

And whoso shall receive one such little child in my name receiveth me. But whoso shall offend one of these little ones which believe in me, it were better for him that a millstone were hanged about his neck, and that he were drowned in the depth of the sea.

Mark 10:13-16

KJV—They brought young children to him, that he should touch them: and his disciples rebuked those that brought them. But when Jesus saw it, he was much displeased, and said unto them, Suffer the little children to come unto me, and forbid them not: for of such is the kingdom of God. Verily I say unto you, Whosoever shall not receive the kingdom of God as a little child, he shall not enter therein. And he took them up in his arms, put his hands upon them, and blessed them.

Protection Promises

A Spectator
in the Battle

*Call upon me in
the day of trouble:
I will deliver thee, and
thou shalt glorify me.*
Psalm 50:15

Thou preparest a table before me
in the presence of mine enemies.
Psalm 23:5

A thousand may fall at your side, and
ten thousand at your right hand, but it
shall not come near you. Only a spectator
shall you be [yourself inaccessible in the
secret place of the Most High] as you
witness the reward of the wicked.
Psalm 91:7-8, AMP

The worst feeling in the world is to feel like you have your back against the wall, surrounded by your circumstances and helpless, vulnerable at any moment to the attack of the enemy.

The good news is that when you are standing on the promises of God's Word, your back is never against the wall. In fact, the promise of God's Word to you is: "The battle is not yours, but the Lord's." God will fight for you.

In your stand for deliverance, don't be confused about who your real enemy is. Your battle is not against flesh and blood. Ephesians 6:12 says, "We wrestle not against *flesh and blood, but against principalities, against powers, against the rulers of the darkness of this world, against spiritual wickedness in high places.*"

The focus of our deliverance is not on those whom Satan has deceived and through whom he may be working. Our focus is on God's love for us and His promises to us. Jesus said, "*No deadly thing shall hurt you*" (Mark 16:18). Psalm 91:13-15 declares: "*Thou shalt tread upon the lion and adder: the young lion and the dragon shalt thou trample under feet. Because he hath set his love upon me, therefore will I deliver him: I will set him on high, because he hath known my name.... I will deliver him, and honour him.*"

If Satan brings a worried thought to your mind, saying, *What if this terrible thing happens?* then you can tell him to talk to God about it. It's in His hands, not yours!

Do what the Israelites did in 2 Chronicles 20. There, the Bible tells us that a multitude of forces were marching against Israel. The army of Israel was so outnumbered, they literally didn't know what to do. So they fasted and prayed until they received a word from God. "*Be not afraid nor dismayed by reason of this great multitude; for the battle is not yours, but God's.*"

Do you know what they did in response to that word? They put together a praise choir! That's right. They appointed singers and praisers and sent them out in front of the army! And when that choir began to sing, the Word tells us that "*the Lord set ambushments against the children of Ammon, Moab,*

A *Spectator in the Battle*

and mount Seir, which were come against Judah; and they were smitten."

When it was all over, not one Israelite had fallen. What's more, the spoil of cattle, goods, garments and other precious things left by their enemies took them three whole days to haul home.

Now that's success! And it all began with trusting God's Word and praising Him in advance for the victory.

The Battle Is the Lord's

Deuteronomy 3:22

KJV—Ye shall not fear them: for the Lord your God he shall fight for you.

AMP—You shall not fear them, for the Lord your God shall fight for you.

Moffatt—Fear them not; it is the Eternal your God who fights for you.

NIV—Do not be afraid of them; the Lord your God himself will fight for you.

1 Samuel 17:47

KJV—The Lord saveth not with sword and spear: for the battle is the Lord's.

AMP—The Lord saves not with sword and spear; for the battle is the Lord's.

Moffatt—The Eternal does not save by sword and spear—the fight is in the Eternal's hands.

NIV—It is not by sword or spear that the Lord saves; for the battle is the Lord's.

2 Chronicles 20:15

KJV—Thus saith the Lord unto you, Be not afraid nor dismayed by reason of this great multitude; for the battle is not yours, but God's.

AMP—The Lord says this to you: Be not afraid or dismayed at this great multitude; for the battle is not yours but God's.

Moffatt—The Eternal's message to you is this: "Fear not, falter not before this vast army; it is for God, not for you, to fight them."

NIV—This is what the Lord says to you: "Do not be afraid or discouraged because of this vast army. For the battle is not yours, but God's."

God Delivers His People

Exodus 14:13-14

KJV—Fear ye not, stand still, and see the salvation of the Lord, which he will show to you today.... The Lord shall fight for you, and ye shall hold your peace.

AMP—Fear not, stand still (firm, confident, undismayed) and see the salvation of the

Lord, which He will work for you today....
The Lord will fight for you, and you shall
hold your peace and remain at rest.

Moffatt—Have no fear, stand firm and
watch how the Eternal will deliver you today.... The Eternal will fight for you, and you
have only to keep still.

NIV—Do not be afraid. Stand firm and you
will see the deliverance the Lord will bring
you today.... The Lord will fight for you; you
need only to be still.

Deuteronomy 1:29-30

KJV—Dread not, neither be afraid of them.
The Lord your God which goeth before
you, he shall fight for you.

AMP—Dread not, neither be afraid of
them. The Lord your God Who goes before
you, He will fight for you.

Moffatt—Dread them not, have no fear of
them. The Eternal your God who goes in
front of you, he will fight for you; he will do
it all for you.

NIV—Do not be terrified; do not be afraid
of them. The Lord your God, who is going
before you, will fight for you.

2 Kings 17:39

KJV—The Lord your God ye shall fear; and
he shall deliver you out of the hand of all
your enemies.

AMP—The Lord your God you shall (reverently) fear; then He will deliver you out of the hand of all your enemies.

Moffatt—Worship the Eternal your God, and he will rescue you from all your foes.

NIV—Worship the Lord your God; it is he who will deliver you from the hand of all your enemies.

1 Chronicles 14:10

KJV—The Lord said unto him [David], Go up; for I will deliver them [the Philistines] into thine hand.

AMP—The Lord said [to David], Go up, and I will deliver them [the Philistines] into your hand.

Moffatt—The Eternal said to him [David], "Attack them, for I will put them [the Philistines] into your hands."

NIV—The Lord answered him [David], "Go, I will hand them [the Philistines] over to you."

Ezra 8:31

KJV—The hand of our God was upon us, and he delivered us from the hand of the enemy, and of such as lay in wait by the way.

Moffatt—The favour of our God was with us, and he kept us safe from the enemy and from any ambush by the road.

NIV—The hand of our God was on us, and he protected us from enemies and bandits along the way.

Jeremiah 1:19

KJV—They shall fight against thee; but they shall not prevail against thee; for I am with thee, saith the Lord, to deliver thee.

Protection Promises

AMP—They shall fight against you, but they shall not finally prevail against you, for I am with you, says the Lord, to deliver you.

Moffatt—They shall attack you, but they shall not overcome you, for I am with you (the Eternal promises) to succour you.

NIV—"They will fight against you but will not overcome you, for I am with you and will rescue you," declares the Lord.

Daniel 6:25-27

KJV—King Darius wrote unto all people, nations, and languages, that dwell in all the earth...I make a decree, That in every dominion of my kingdom men tremble and fear before the God of Daniel: for he is the living God, and stedfast for ever, and his kingdom that which shall not be destroyed, and his dominion shall be even unto the end. He delivereth and rescueth, and he worketh signs and wonders in heaven and in earth, who hath delivered Daniel from the power of the lions.

AMP—King Darius wrote to all peoples, nations, and languages [in his realm] that dwell in all the earth…I make a decree, That in all my royal dominion men tremble and fear before the God of Daniel, for He is the living God, enduring and steadfast for ever, and His kingdom shall not be destroyed, and His dominion shall be even to the end [of the world]. He is a savior and deliverer, and He works signs and wonders in the heavens and on the earth, Who has delivered Daniel from the power of the lions.

Moffatt—King Darius wrote to all nations, races, and folk of every tongue, who dwell in all the world…"I pass a decree that in all the realm I rule men shall tremble in fear before the God of Daniel, for he is the living God, for ever he endures, his kingdom never shall be overthrown, and his dominion has no end: he saves and rescues, he does signal acts in heaven and earth: and he has rescued Daniel from the power of lions."

NIV—King Darius wrote to all the peoples, nations and men of every language throughout the land…"I issue a decree that in every part of my kingdom people must fear and reverence the God of Daniel. For he is the living God and he endures forever; his kingdom will not be destroyed, his dominion will never end. He rescues and he saves; he performs signs and wonders in the heavens and on the earth. He has rescued Daniel from the power of the lions."

An Enemy to Your Enemies

Deuteronomy 23:14

KJV—The Lord thy God walketh in the midst of thy camp, to deliver thee, and to give up thine enemies before thee.

AMP—The Lord your God walks in the midst of your camp to deliver you and to give up your enemies before you.

NIV—The Lord your God moves about in your camp to protect you and to deliver your enemies to you.

NAS—The Lord your God walks in the midst of your camp to deliver you and to defeat your enemies before you.

Psalm 18:43

KJV—Thou hast delivered me from the strivings of the people; and thou hast made me the head of the heathen: a people whom I have not known shall serve me.

AMP—You have delivered me from strivings of the people; You made me the head of the nations; a people I had not known served me.

NIV—You have delivered me from the attacks of the people; you have made me the head of nations; people I did not know are subject to me.

NAS—Thou hast delivered me from the contentions of the people; Thou hast placed me as head of the nations; A people whom I have not known serve me.

Psalm 35:19

KJV—Let not them that are mine enemies wrongfully rejoice over me: neither let them wink with the eye that hate me without a cause.

AMP—Let not those who are my foes wrongfully rejoice over me; neither let them wink with the eye who hate me without cause.

Moffatt—Let not my foes rejoice over me wrongfully, let not my wanton haters wink maliciously!

NIV—Let not those gloat over me who are my enemies without cause; let not those who hate me without reason maliciously wink the eye.

Psalm 41:11

KJV—I know that thou favourest me, because mine enemy doth not triumph over me.

AMP—I know that You favor and delight in me, because my enemy does not triumph over me.

Moffatt—I shall be sure thou carest for me, when my foe fails to triumph over me.

NAS—I know that Thou art pleased with me, Because my enemy does not shout in triumph over me.

Psalm 44:7

KJV—Thou hast saved us from our enemies, and hast put them to shame that hated us.

AMP—You have saved us from our foes, and have put them to shame who hate us.

NIV—You give us victory over our enemies, you put our adversaries to shame.

NAS—Thou hast saved us from our adversaries, And Thou has put to shame those who hate us.

Psalm 57:3

KJV—He shall send from heaven, and save me from the reproach of him that would swallow me up... God shall send forth his mercy and his truth.

AMP—He will send from Heaven and save me from the slanders and reproaches of him who would trample me down or swallow me up, and put him to shame.... God will send forth His mercy and loving-kindness and His truth and faithfulness.

Moffatt—God send me help from heaven! God send his love and loyalty, discomfiting those who would trample me down!

NIV—He sends from heaven and saves me, rebuking those who hotly pursue me. God sends his love and his faithfulness.

Psalm 68:1

KJV—Let God arise, let his enemies be scattered: let them also that hate him flee before him.

A Spectator in the Battle

AMP—God is [already] beginning to arise, and His enemies to scatter; let them also who hate Him flee before Him!

Moffatt—When God stirs, his enemies scatter, those who hate him fly before him.

NIV—May God arise, may his enemies be scattered; may his foes flee before him.

Psalm 109:29

KJV—Let mine adversaries be clothed with shame, and let them cover themselves with their own confusion, as with a mantle.

AMP—Let my adversaries be clothed with shame and dishonor, and let them cover themselves with their own disgrace and confusion, as with a robe.

Moffatt—May my opponents be covered with disgrace, robed in their own dishonour!

NIV—My accusers will be clothed with disgrace and wrapped in shame as in a cloak.

Psalm 140:1, 4

KJV—Deliver me, O Lord, from the evil man: preserve me from the violent man.... Keep me, O Lord, from the hands of the wicked; preserve me from the violent man; who have purposed to overthrow my goings.

AMP—Deliver me, O Lord, from the evil man; preserve me from the violent man.... Keep me, O Lord, from the hands of the wicked; preserve me from the violent men, who have purposed to thrust aside my steps.

Moffatt—From evil men deliver me, O Eternal, save me from violent men.... Preserve me, O Eternal, from the grip of the ungodly, save me from outrageous men, who plan to overthrow me.

NIV—Rescue me, O Lord, from evil men; protect me from men of violence.... Keep me, O Lord, from the hands of the wicked; protect me from men of violence who plan to trip my feet.

Jeremiah 20:11

KJV—The Lord is with me as a mighty terrible one: therefore my persecutors shall stumble, and they shall not prevail: they shall be greatly ashamed; for they shall not prosper.

AMP—The Lord is with me as a mighty and terrible one; therefore my persecutors will stumble, and they will not overcome me. They will be utterly put to shame, for they will not deal wisely or prosper [in their schemes].

Moffatt—I have the Eternal on my side, a dread and doughty champion! My persecutors shall collapse and miss their aim; bitter shall be their shame over their failure.

NIV—The Lord is with me like a mighty warrior; so my persecutors will stumble and not prevail. They will fail and be thoroughly disgraced.

Zechariah 2:8-9

KJV—Thus saith the Lord of hosts...He that toucheth you toucheth the apple of his eye. For, behold, I will shake mine hand upon them, and they shall be a spoil to their servants.

AMP—Thus said the Lord of hosts...He who touches you touches the apple or pupil of His eye: Behold, I will swing my hand over them, and they shall become plunder for those who served them.

Moffatt—The Lord of hosts declares (for he who touches you touches the apple of the Eternal's eye), I will swing my hand over them, and they shall be plundered by their victims.

NIV—This is what the Lord Almighty says... "Whoever touches you touches the apple of his eye—I will surely raise my hand against them so that their slaves will plunder them."

Your Shield and Strength

2 Samuel 22:33-34

KJV—God is my strength and power: and he maketh my way perfect. He maketh my feet like hinds' feet: and setteth me upon my high places.

AMP—God is my strong fortress; He guides the blameless in His way and sets him free. He makes my feet like the hinds' [firm and able]; He sets me secure and confident upon the heights.

Moffatt—God is my stronghold, God is a perfect guide to me. He makes me nimble as a deer, and sets me on the height.

NIV—It is God who arms me with strength and makes my way perfect. He makes my feet like the feet of a deer; he enables me to stand on the heights.

Psalm 3:3

KJV—Thou, O Lord, art a shield for me; my glory, and the lifter up of mine head.

AMP—You, O Lord, are a shield for me, my glory, and the lifter up of my head.

Moffatt—Thou shieldest me, O thou Eternal, in triumph, thou whom I do glorify!

NIV—You are a shield around me, O Lord; you bestow glory on me and lift up my head.

Psalm 18:35

KJV—Thou hast also given me the shield of thy salvation: and thy right hand hath holden me up, and thy gentleness hath made me great.

AMP—You have also given me the shield of Your salvation, and Your right hand has held me up; Your gentleness and condescension have made me great.

Moffatt—Thou hast shielded me with thine aid, thy right hand holds me up; thine answers to prayer have raised me.

NIV—You give me your shield of victory, and your right hand sustains me; you stoop down to make me great.

Psalm 18:39

KJV—Thou hast girded me with strength unto the battle: thou hast subdued under me those that rose up against me.

AMP—You have girded me with strength for the battle; You have subdued under me and caused to bow down those who rose up against me.

Moffatt—Thou hast braced me for the fray; thou makest my assailants drop before me.

NIV—You armed me with strength for battle; you made my adversaries bow at my feet.

Psalm 119:114

KJV—Thou art my hiding place and my shield: I hope in thy word.

AMP—You are my hiding place and my shield; I hope in Your word.

Moffatt—I await thy promise, thou my shield and shelter.

NIV—You are my refuge and my shield; I have put my hope in your word.

Psalm 140:7

KJV—O God the Lord, the strength of my salvation, thou hast covered my head in the day of battle.

AMP—O God the Lord, the strength of my salvation, You have covered my head in the day of battle.

Moffatt—Eternal One, my Lord, my saving strength, who screenest me against attack.

NIV—O Sovereign Lord, my strong deliverer, who shields my head in the day of battle.

Proverbs 30:5

KJV—Every word of God is pure: he is a shield unto them that put their trust in him.

AMP—Every word of God is tried and purified; He is a shield to those who trust and take refuge in Him.

Moffatt—God's promises are all tried and true; those who shelter beside him he shields.

NIV—Every word of God is flawless; he is a shield to those who take refuge in him.

Ephesians 6:10-18

KJV—Be strong in the Lord, and in the power of his might. Put on the whole armour of God, that ye may be able to stand against the wiles of the devil. For we wrestle not against flesh and blood, but against principalities, against powers, against the rulers of the darkness of this world, against spiritual wickedness in high places. Wherefore take unto you the whole armour of God, that ye may be able to withstand in the evil day, and having done all, to stand. Stand therefore, having your loins girt about with truth, and having on the breastplate of righteousness; And your feet shod with the preparation of the gospel of peace; Above all, taking the shield of faith, wherewith ye shall be able to quench all the fiery darts of the wicked. And take the helmet of salvation, and the sword of the Spirit, which is the word of God: Praying always with all prayer and supplication in the Spirit, and watching thereunto with all perseverance and supplication for all saints.

AMP—Be strong in the Lord—be empowered through your union with Him; draw your strength from Him—that strength which His [boundless] might provides. Put on God's whole armor—the armor of a heavy-armed soldier, which God supplies— that you may be able successfully to stand up against [all] the strategies and the deceits of the devil. For we are not wrestling with flesh and blood—contending only with physical opponents—but against the despotisms, against the powers, against [the master spirits who are] the world rulers of this present darkness, against the spirit forces of wickedness in the heavenly (supernatural) sphere. Therefore put on God's complete armor, that you may be able to resist and stand your ground on the evil day [of danger], and having done all [the crisis demands], to stand [firmly in your place]. Stand therefore—hold your ground— having tightened the belt of truth around your loins, and having put on the breastplate of integrity and of moral rectitude and right standing with God; And having shod your feet in preparation [to face the enemy with the firm-footed stability, the promptness and the readiness produced by the good news] of the Gospel of peace. Lift up over all the (covering) shield of saving faith, upon which you can quench all the flaming missiles of the wicked [one]. And take the helmet of salvation and the sword the Spirit wields, which is the Word of God. Pray at all times—on every occasion, in every season—in the Spirit, with all [manner of] prayer and entreaty. To that end keep alert and watch with strong purpose and perseverance, interceding in behalf of all the saints (God's consecrated people).

NIV—Be strong in the Lord and in his mighty power. Put on the full armor of God so that you can take your stand against the devil's schemes. For our struggle is not against flesh and blood, but against the rulers, against the authorities, against the powers of this dark world and against the spiritual forces of evil in the heavenly realms. Therefore put on the full armor of God, so that when the day of evil comes, you may be able to stand your ground, and after you have done everything, to stand. Stand firm then, with the belt of truth buckled around your waist, with the breastplate of righteousness in place, and with your feet fitted with the readiness that comes from the gospel of peace. In addition to all this, take up the shield of faith, with which you can extinguish all the flaming arrows of the evil one. Take the helmet of salvation and the sword of the Spirit, which is the word of God. And pray in the Spirit on all

A *Spectator in the* Battle

occasions with all kinds of prayers and requests. With this in mind, be alert and always keep on praying for all the saints.

Spectator in the Battle

Psalm 23:5

KJV—Thou preparest a table before me in the presence of mine enemies: thou anointest my head with oil; my cup runneth over.

AMP—You prepare a table before me in the presence of my enemies; You anoint my head with oil; my [brimming] cup runs over.

Moffatt—Thou art my host, spreading a feast for me, while my foes have to look on! Thou hast poured oil upon my head, my cup is brimming over.

Psalm 55:16, 18

NIV—The Lord saves me.... He ransoms me unharmed from the battle waged against me, even though many oppose me.

KJV—The Lord shall save me.... He hath delivered my soul in peace from the battle that was against me: for there were many with me.

AMP—The Lord will save me.... He has redeemed my life in peace from the battle that was against me [so that none came near me], for they were many who strove with me.

Moffatt—The Eternal helps me.... [He will] give me peace and freedom from this strife, from the host of foes around me.

Psalm 91:7-13

KJV—A thousand shall fall at thy side, and ten thousand at thy right hand; but it shall not come nigh thee. Only with thine eyes shalt thou behold and see the reward of the wicked.

A *Spectator in the Battle*

AMP—A thousand may fall at your side, and ten thousand at your right hand, but it shall not come near you. Only a spectator shall you be [yourself inaccessible in the secret place of the Most High] as you witness the reward of the wicked.

TLB—Though a thousand fall at my side, though ten thousand are dying around me, the evil will not touch me. I will see how the wicked are punished but I will not share it.

Psalm 138:7

KJV—Though I walk in the midst of trouble, thou wilt revive me: thou shalt stretch forth thine hand against the wrath of mine enemies, and thy right hand shall save me.

AMP—Though I walk in the midst of trouble, You will revive me; You will stretch forth Your hand against the wrath of my enemies, and Your right hand will save me.

Moffatt—Though I must pass through the thick of trouble, thou wilt preserve me; thy hand shall fall upon my angry foes, thy right hand rescues me.

NIV—Though I walk in the midst of trouble, you preserve my life; you stretch out your hand against the anger of my foes, with your right hand you save me.

Isaiah 43:1-3

KJV—Fear not: for I have redeemed thee, I have called thee by thy name; thou art mine. When thou passest through the waters, I will be with thee; and through the rivers, they shall not overflow thee: when thou walkest through the fire, thou shalt not be burned; neither shall the flame kindle upon thee. For I am the Lord thy God, the Holy One of Israel, thy Saviour.

AMP—Fear not, for I have redeemed you—ransomed you by paying a price instead of leaving you captives; I have called you by your name, you are Mine. When you pass through the waters I will be with you, and through the rivers they shall not over-whelm you; when you walk through the fire you shall not be burned or scorched, nor shall the flame kindle upon you. For I am the Lord your God, the Holy One of Israel, your Savior.

Moffatt—Fear not, for I redeem you, I claim you, you are mine. I will be with you when you pass through waters, no rivers shall overflow you; when you pass through fire, you shall not be scorched, no flames shall burn you. For I the Eternal am your God, Israel's Majestic One is your deliverer.

NIV—Fear not, for I have redeemed you; I have summoned you by name; you are mine. When you pass through the waters, I will be with you; and when you pass through the rivers, they will not sweep over you. When you walk through the fire, you will not be burned; the flames will not set you ablaze. For I am the Lord, your God, the Holy One of Israel, your Savior.

Isaiah 54:14-15

KJV—In righteousness shalt thou be established: thou shalt be far from oppression; for thou shalt not fear: and from terror; for it shall not come near thee. Behold, they shall surely gather together, but not by me: whosoever shall gather together against thee shall fall for thy sake.

AMP—You shall establish yourself on righteousness—right, in conformity with God's will and order; you shall be far even from the thought of oppression or destruction, for you shall not fear; and from terror, for it shall not come near you. Behold, they may gather together and stir up strife, but it is not from Me. Whoever stirs up strife against you shall fall away to you.

NIV—In righteousness you will be established: Tyranny will be far from you; you will have nothing to fear. Terror will be far removed; it will not come near you. If anyone does attack you, it will not be my doing; whoever attacks you will surrender to you.

NAS—In righteousness you will be established; You will be far from oppression, for you will not fear; And from terror, for it will not come near you. If anyone fiercely assails you it will not be from Me. Whoever assails you will fall because of you.

Matthew 10:17, 19-20

AMP—Be on guard against the men [whose way or nature is to act in opposition to God]; for they will deliver you up to councils.... But when they deliver you up, do not be anxious about how or what you are to speak; for what you are to say will be given you in that very hour and moment. For it is not you who are speaking, but the Spirit of your Father speaking through you.

KJV—Beware of men: for they will deliver you up to the councils.... But when they deliver you up, take no thought how or what ye shall speak: for it shall be given you in that same hour what ye shall speak. For it is not ye that speak, but the Spirit of your Father which speaketh in you.

Weymouth—Beware of men; for they will deliver you up to appear before Sanhedrins... But when they have delivered you up, have no anxiety as to how you shall speak or what you shall say; for at that very time it shall be given you what to say; for it is not you who will speak: it will be the Spirit of your Father speaking through you.

NAS—Beware of men; for they will deliver you up to the courts.... But when they deliver you up, do not become anxious about how or what you will speak; for it shall be given you in that hour what you are to speak. For it is not you who speak, but it is the Spirit of your Father who speaks in you.

A *Spectator*
in the Battle

Enforcing
Jesus' Victory

All power is given
unto me in heaven
and in earth.
Go ye therefore....
Matthew 28:18-19

Thanks be to God, which giveth us the victory through our Lord Jesus Christ.

1 Corinthians 15:57

One of our strongest positions of protection is stepping out in faith, moving against every lie and attack of the enemy. God has equipped you with His faith, His Word and His anointing for this. You have not only a strong defense against Satan, but also the authority and power to rise up and enforce the victory Jesus won for all mankind at the cross.

Think about it. Since Jesus has already defeated Satan, we as believers aren't going somewhere to do battle. We are going somewhere to do victory! We are a part of the army of Jesus, the Anointed One. We're on a mission to occupy this earth and enforce the devil's defeat until Jesus returns.

You won't experience the fullness of God's protection and the victory Jesus won over Satan until you step out in faith and by your words and actions take authority over every manifestation of darkness and death.

See Satan as he really is—powerless against the Word of God. Understand that he has no power except the power of deceit and of agreement in those who believe his lies. Recognize that, for the believer who will speak the Word of God in faith in the face of the devil's lies, Satan is bound to always respond in the same way: "*Resist the devil, and he will flee*" (James 4:7).

Don't waste time worrying about the devil. Take authority over him. Step out in every way God has equipped you with His faith, His Word and His anointing. Bind the evil spirits that try to destroy your home, your church and your nation. Loose God's Word in the earth and enforce it with the Name of Jesus.

Use your faith to enforce the devil's defeat and Christ's victory.

Enforce His Victory

Genesis 14:20

KJV—Blessed be the most high God, which hath delivered thine enemies into thy hand.

AMP—Blessed, praised and glorified be God Most High Who has given your foes into your hand!

Moffatt—Blessed be God Most High, who has put your foes into your hand!

NIV—Blessed be God Most High, who delivered your enemies into your hand.

Leviticus 26:8

KJV—Five of you shall chase an hundred, and an hundred of you shall put ten thousand to flight: and your enemies shall fall before you.

AMP—Five of you shall chase a hundred, and a hundred of you shall put ten thousand to flight; your enemies shall fall before you.

Moffatt—Five of you shall chase a hundred, a hundred shall chase ten thousand, till your enemies are cut down before you.

NIV—Five of you will chase a hundred, and a hundred of you will chase ten thousand, and your enemies will fall...before you.

Protection Promises

Deuteronomy 6:17-19

KJV—Ye shall diligently keep the commandments of the Lord your God, and his testimonies, and his statutes, which he hath commanded thee. And thou shalt do that which is right and good in the sight of the Lord: that it may be well with thee, and that thou mayest go in and possess the good land which the Lord sware unto thy fathers, To cast out all thine enemies from before thee, as the Lord hath spoken.

AMP—You shall diligently keep the commandments of the Lord your God, and His exhortations, and His statutes, which He commanded you. And you shall do what is right and good in the sight of the Lord, that it may go well with you, and that you may go in and possess the good land which the Lord swore to give to your fathers, To cast out all your enemies from before you, as the Lord has promised.

NIV—Be sure to keep the commands of the Lord your God and the stipulations and decrees he has given you. Do what is right and good in the Lord's sight, so that it may go well with you and you may go in and take over the good land that the Lord promised on oath to your forefathers, thrusting out all your enemies before you, as the Lord said.

Deuteronomy 20:4

KJV—The Lord your God is he that goeth with you, to fight for you against your enemies, to save you.

AMP—The Lord your God is He Who goes with you, to fight for you against your enemies, to save you.

Moffatt—The Eternal your God goes with you, to fight for you against your enemies and to give you the victory.

NIV—The Lord your God is the one who goes with you to fight for you against your enemies to give you victory.

2 Samuel 22:40

KJV—Thou hast girded me with strength to battle: them that rose up against me hast thou subdued under me.

AMP—You girded me with strength for the battle; those who rose up against me You subdued under me.

NIV—You armed me with strength for battle; you made my adversaries bow at my feet.

NAS—Thou hast girded me with strength for battle; Thou has subdued under me those who rose up against me.

2 Chronicles 20:17

KJV—Ye shall not need to fight in this battle: set yourselves, stand ye still, and see the salvation of the Lord...Fear not, nor be dismayed; to morrow go out against them: for the Lord will be with you.

AMP—You shall not need to fight in this battle; take your position, stand still, and see the deliverance of the Lord [Who is] with you...Fear not, nor be dismayed; tomorrow go out against them, for the Lord is with you.

NIV—You will not have to fight this battle. Take up your positions; stand firm and see the deliverance the Lord will give you...Do not be afraid; do not be discouraged. Go out to face them tomorrow, and the Lord will be with you.

Psalm 18:34

KJV—He [God] teacheth my hands to war, so that a bow of steel is broken by mine arms.

AMP—He [God] teaches my hands to war, so that my arms bend a bow of bronze.

Moffatt—He [God] trains me how to fight, till I can bend a bow of bronze.

NIV—He [God] trains my hands for battle; my arms can bend a bow of bronze.

Psalm 108:13

KJV—Through God we shall do valiantly.

AMP—Through and with God we shall do valiantly.

Moffatt—With God we shall do bravely.

NIV—With God we will gain the victory.

Psalm 110:1-2

KJV—The Lord said unto my Lord, Sit thou at my right hand, until I make thine enemies thy footstool. The Lord shall send the rod of thy strength out of Zion: rule thou in the midst of thine enemies.

AMP—The Lord (God) says to my Lord [the Messiah], Sit You at My right hand, until I make Your adversaries Your footstool. The Lord will send forth from Zion the scepter of Your strength; rule, then, in the midst of Your foes.

NIV—The Lord says to my Lord: "Sit at my right hand until I make your enemies a footstool for your feet." The Lord will extend your mighty scepter from Zion; you will rule in the midst of your enemies.

NAS—The Lord says to my Lord: "Sit at My right hand, Until I make Thine enemies a footstool for Thy feet." The Lord will stretch forth Thy strong scepter from Zion, saying, "Rule in the midst of Thine enemies."

Isaiah 59:19-21

AMP—When the enemy shall come in, like a flood the Spirit of the Lord will lift up a standard against him and put him to flight—for He will come like a rushing stream which the breath of the Lord drives. He shall come as a Redeemer to Zion, and to those in Jacob (Israel) who turn from transgression, says the Lord. As for Me, this is My covenant or league with them, says the Lord: My Spirit Who is upon you [and Who writes the law of God inwardly in the heart], and My words which I have put in your mouth, shall not depart out of your mouth, or out of the mouth of your [true, spiritual] children, or out of the mouth of your children's children, says the Lord, from henceforth and for ever.

KJV—When the enemy shall come in, like a flood the Spirit of the Lord shall lift up a standard against him. And the Redeemer shall come to Zion, and unto them that turn from transgression in Jacob, saith the Lord. As for me, this is my covenant with them, saith the Lord; My spirit that is upon thee, and my words which I have put in thy mouth, shall not depart out of thy mouth, nor out of the mouth of thy seed, nor out of the mouth of thy seed's seed, saith the Lord, from henceforth and for ever.

NKJV—When the enemy comes in, like a flood The Spirit of the Lord will lift up a standard against him. "The Redeemer will come to Zion, And to those who turn from transgression in Jacob," Says the Lord. "As for Me," says the Lord, "this is My covenant with them: My Spirit who is upon you, and My words which I have put in your mouth, shall not depart from your mouth, nor from the mouth of your descendants, nor from the mouth of your descendants' descendants," says the Lord, "from this time and forevermore."

Luke 10:19

KJV—Behold, I give unto you power to tread on serpents and scorpions, and over all the power of the enemy: and nothing shall by any means hurt you.

AMP—Behold! I have given you authority and power to trample upon serpents and scorpions, and (physical and mental strength and ability) over all the power that the enemy [possesses], and nothing shall in any way harm you.

Weymouth—I have given you power to tread serpents and scorpions under foot, and to trample on all the power of the enemy; and in no case shall anything do you harm.

NIV—I have given you authority to trample on snakes and scorpions and to overcome all the power of the enemy; nothing will harm you.

Romans 8:31

KJV—If God be for us, who can be against us?

AMP—If God be for us, who [can be] against us?—Who can be our foe, if God is on our side?

Weymouth—If God is for us, who can be against us?

TLB—If God is on our side, who can ever be against us?

2 Corinthians 10:3-5

KJV—Though we walk in the flesh, we do not war after the flesh: (For the weapons of our warfare are not carnal, but mighty through God to the pulling down of strong holds;) Casting down imaginations, and every high thing that exalteth itself against the knowledge of God, and bringing into captivity every thought to the obedience of Christ.

AMP—Though we walk [live] in the flesh, we are not carrying on our warfare according to the flesh and using mere human weapons. For the weapons of our warfare are not physical (weapons of flesh and blood), but they are mighty before God for the overthrow and destruction of strongholds, [Inasmuch as we] refute arguments and theories and reasonings and every proud and lofty thing that sets itself up against the (true) knowledge of God; and we lead every thought and purpose away captive into the obedience of Christ, the Messiah, the Anointed One.

NIV—Though we live in the world, we do not wage war as the world does. The weapons we fight with are not the weapons of the world. On the contrary, they have divine power to demolish strongholds. We demolish arguments and every pretension that sets itself up against the knowledge of God, and we take captive every thought to make it obedient to Christ.

Ephesians 1:15-23

KJV—Wherefore I also, after I heard of your faith in the Lord Jesus, and love unto all the saints, Cease not to give thanks for you, making mention of you in my prayers; That the God of our Lord Jesus Christ, the Father of glory, may give unto you the spirit of wisdom and revelation in the knowledge of him: The eyes of your understanding being enlightened; that ye may know what is the hope of his calling, and what the riches of the glory of his inheritance in the saints, And what is the exceeding greatness of his power to us-ward who believe, according to the working of his mighty power, Which he wrought in Christ, when he raised him from the dead, and set him at his own right hand in the heavenly places, Far above all principality, and power, and might, and dominion, and every name that is named, not only in this world, but also in that which is to come: And hath put all things under his feet, and gave him to be the head over all things to the church, Which is his body, the fulness of him that filleth all in all.

NIV—For this reason, ever since I heard about your faith in the Lord Jesus and your love for all the saints, I have not stopped giving thanks for you, remembering you in my prayers. I keep asking that the God of our Lord Jesus Christ, the glorious Father, may give you the Spirit of wisdom and revelation, so that you may know him better. I pray also that the eyes of your heart may be enlightened in order that you may know the hope to which he has called you, the riches of his glorious inheritance in the saints, and his incomparably great power for us who believe. That power is like the working of his mighty strength, which he exerted in Christ when he raised him from the dead and seated him at his right hand in the heavenly realms, far above all rule and authority, power and dominion, and every title that can be given, not only in the present age but also in the one to come. And God placed all things under his feet and appointed him to be head over everything for the church, which is his body, the fullness of him who fills everything in every way.

James 4:7

KJV—Submit yourselves therefore to God. Resist the devil, and he will flee from you.

AMP—Be subject to God.—Stand firm against the devil; resist him and he will flee from you.

Weymouth—Submit therefore to God: resist the devil, and he will flee from you.

NIV—Submit yourselves, then, to God. Resist the devil, and he will flee from you.

1 John 4:3-4

KJV—Every spirit that confesseth not that Jesus Christ is come in the flesh is not of God: and this is that spirit of antichrist, whereof ye have heard that it should come; and even now already is it in the world. Ye are of God, little children, and have overcome them: because greater is he that is in you, than he that is in the world.

AMP—Every spirit which does not acknowledge and confess that Jesus Christ has come in the flesh [but would annul, destroy, sever, disunite Him] is not of God—does not proceed from Him. This [non-confession] is the [spirit] of antichrist, [of] which you heard that it was coming, and now it is already in the world. Little children, you are of God—you belong to Him—and have [already] defeated and overcome them [the agents of antichrist], because He Who lives in you is greater (mightier) than he who is in the world.

Weymouth—Jesus Christ has come in the flesh...and...no spirit is from God which does not acknowledge this about Jesus. Such is the spirit of the antichrist; you have heard that it is to come, and now it is already in the world. You, dear children, are God's children, and have overcome them; for greater is He who is in you than he who is in the world.

NIV—Every spirit that does not acknowledge Jesus is not from God. This is the spirit of the antichrist, which you have heard is coming and even now is already in the world. You, dear children, are from God and have overcome them, because the one who is in you is greater than the one who is in the world.

1 John 5:4

KJV—Whatsoever is born of God overcometh the world: and this is the victory that overcometh the world, even our faith.

AMP—Whatever is born of God is victorious over the world; and this is the victory that conquers the world, even our faith.

Weymouth—Every thing that is born of God overcomes the world; and the victory which has overcome the world is our faith.

NIV—Everyone born of God overcomes the world. This is the victory that has overcome the world, even our faith.

Act in His Name

Psalm 20:7-8

KJV—Some trust in chariots, and some in horses: but we will remember the name of the Lord our God. They are brought down and fallen: but we are risen, and stand upright.

AMP—Some trust in and boast of chariots, and some of horses; but we will trust in and boast of the name of the Lord our God. They are bowed down and fallen; but we are risen and stand upright.

Moffatt—Some pride themselves on chariots, some on horses, but our pride is our God the Eternal; the foe must bow and fall, we rise and stand erect.

NIV—Some trust in chariots and some in horses, but we trust in the name of the Lord our God. They are brought to their knees and fall, but we rise up and stand firm.

Psalm 89:21-24

KJV—My hand shall be established: mine arm also shall strengthen him. The enemy shall not exact upon him; nor the son of wickedness afflict him... My faithfulness and my mercy shall be with him: and in my name shall his horn be exalted.

AMP—My hand shall be established and ever abide, My arm also shall strengthen him. The enemy shall not exact from him or do him violence or outwit him, or the wicked afflict and humble him... My faithfulness and My mercy and loving-kindness shall be with him, and in My name shall his horn be exalted [great power and prosperity shall be conferred upon him].

NIV—My hand will sustain him; surely my arm will strengthen him. No enemy will subject him to tribute; no wicked man will oppress him... My faithful love will be with him, and through my name his horn will be exalted.

Psalm 124:2-8

KJV—If it had not been the Lord who was on our side, when men rose up against us: Then they had swallowed us up quick, when their wrath was kindled against us: Then the waters had overwhelmed us, the stream had gone over our soul: Then the proud waters had gone over our soul. Blessed be the Lord, who hath not given us as a prey to their teeth. Our soul is escaped as a bird out of the snare of the fowlers: the snare is broken, and we are escaped. Our help is in the name of the Lord, who made heaven and earth.

AMP—If it had not been the Lord Who was on our side, when men rose up against us, Then they would have quickly swallowed us up alive, when their wrath was kindled against us; Then the waters would have overwhelmed us and swept us away, the torrent would have gone over us; Then the proud waters would have gone over us. Blessed be the Lord, Who has not given us as prey to their teeth! We are like a bird escaped from the snare of the fowlers; the snare is broken, and we have escaped! Our help is in the name of the Lord Who made Heaven and earth.

Moffatt—Had not the Eternal been upon our side, when men rose to attack us, they would have swallowed us alive, so fierce their anger flamed; the floods would have swept us away, the streams would have surged over us, surging clean over us, with proud, wild waves. But, blessed be the Eternal! he did not leave us for their teeth to tear; we escaped like a bird from the fowler's snare—the snare broke, we escaped! Our help lies in the Eternal, who made heaven and earth!

Enforcing Jesus' Victory

Mark 16:16-18

KJV—He that believeth and is baptized shall be saved.... And these signs shall follow them that believe; In my name shall they cast out devils; they shall speak with new tongues; They shall take up serpents; and if they drink any deadly thing, it shall not hurt them; they shall lay hands on the sick, and they shall recover.

AMP—He who believes—[that is,] who adheres to and trusts in and relies on the Gospel and Him Whom it sets forth—and is baptized will be saved [from the penalty of eternal death].... And these attesting signs will accompany those who believe: in My name they will drive out demons; they will speak in new languages; They will pick up serpents, and [even] if they drink anything deadly, it will not hurt them; they will lay their hands on the sick, and they will get well.

Weymouth—He who believes and is baptized shall be saved.... And signs shall attend those who believe, even such as these: by my name they shall expel demons; they shall speak new languages; they shall take up venomous snakes; and even if they drink any deadly poison, it shall do them no harm whatever; they shall lay their hands on the sick, and these shall recover.

NIV—Whoever believes and is baptized will be saved.... And these signs will accompany those who believe: In my name they will drive out demons; they will speak in new tongues; they will pick up snakes with their hands; and when they drink deadly poison, it will not hurt them at all; they will place their hands on sick people, and they will get well.

Acts 2:21

KJV—Whosoever shall call on the name of the Lord shall be saved.

Acts 3:12-13, 16

KJV—When Peter saw it, he answered unto the people, Ye men of Israel, why marvel ye at this? or why look ye so earnestly on us, as though by our own power or holiness we had made this man to walk? The God of Abraham, and of Isaac, and of Jacob, the God of our fathers, hath glorified his Son Jesus.... And his name through faith in his name hath made this man strong, whom ye see and know: yea, the faith which is by him hath given him this perfect soundness in the presence of you all.

Romans 10:13-15

KJV—Whosoever shall call upon the name of the Lord shall be saved. How then shall they call on him in whom they have not believed? and how shall they believe in him of whom they have not heard? and how shall they hear without a preacher? And how shall they preach, except they be sent? as it is written, How beautiful are the feet of them that preach the gospel of peace, and bring glad tidings of good things!

Enjoy His Peace

Exodus 33:14

KJV—My presence shall go with thee, and I will give thee rest.

AMP—My presence shall go with you, and I will give you rest.

Moffatt—My presence shall go with you, and I will settle you safe.

NIV—My Presence will go with you, and I will give you rest.

Leviticus 25:18-19

KJV—Ye shall do my statutes, and keep my judgments, and do them; and ye shall dwell in the land in safety. And the land shall yield her fruit, and ye shall eat your fill, and dwell therein in safety.

AMP—You shall do and give effect to My statutes, and keep My ordinances and perform them; and you will dwell in the land in safety. The land shall yield its fruit; you shall eat your fill, and dwell there in safety.

Moffatt—Obey my rules, then, and follow my regulations obediently; so shall you live in the land securely: the land shall yield its crops, and you shall eat your fill and dwell there securely.

NIV—Follow my decrees and be careful to obey my laws, and you will live safely in the land. Then the land will yield its fruit, and you will eat your fill and live there in safety.

Leviticus 26:6

KJV—I will give peace in the land, and ye shall lie down, and none shall make you afraid.

AMP—I will give peace in the land; you shall lie down, and none shall fill you with dread or make you afraid.

Moffatt—I will grant you peace in your land, till you rest with none to scare you.

NIV—I will grant peace in the land, and you will lie down and no one will make you afraid.

Deuteronomy 25:19

KJV—When the Lord thy God hath given thee rest from all thine enemies round about, in the land which the Lord thy God giveth thee for an inheritance to possess it...thou shalt not forget it.

AMP—When the Lord your God has given you rest from all your enemies round about, in the land which the Lord your God gives you to possess for an inheritance...you must not forget it.

Moffatt—When the Eternal your God has given you rest from all your foes around, in the land which the Eternal your God assigns to you as your possession...do not forget that.

NIV—When the Lord your God gives you rest from all the enemies around you in the land he is giving you to possess as an inheritance...Do not forget!

Deuteronomy 33:12

KJV—The beloved of the Lord shall dwell in safety by him; and the Lord shall cover him all the day long, and he shall dwell between his shoulders.

AMP—The beloved of the Lord shall dwell in safety by Him; He covers him all the day long, and makes His dwelling between his shoulders.

Moffatt—The Eternal's darling, he lives ever in security; the Most High encircles him, seated upon his slopes.

NIV—Let the beloved of the Lord rest secure in him, for he shields him all day long, and the one the Lord loves rests between his shoulders.

Psalm 18:18-19

KJV—The Lord was my stay. He brought me forth also into a large place; he delivered me, because he delighted in me.

AMP—The Lord was my stay and support. He brought me forth also into a large place; He was delivering me, because He was pleased with me and delighted in me.

Moffatt—The Eternal comes to my support and sets me free, in a clear space; as he delights in me, he rescues me.

NIV—The Lord was my support. He brought me out into a spacious place; he rescued me because he delighted in me.

Psalm 31:8

KJV—[Thou] hast not shut me up into the hand of the enemy: thou hast set my feet in a large room.

AMP—You have not given me into the hand of the enemy; You have set my feet in a broad place.

Moffatt—[Thou] hast not left me in the clutches of my foes, but hast set me at liberty.

NIV—You have not handed me over to the enemy but have set my feet in a spacious place.

Proverbs 1:33

KJV—Whoso hearkeneth unto me shall dwell safely, and shall be quiet from fear of evil.

AMP—Whoso hearkens to me [Wisdom], shall dwell securely and in confident trust, and shall be quiet without fear or dread of evil.

Moffatt—Safe he lives who listens to me; from fear of harm he shall be wholly free.

NIV—Whoever listens to me will live in safety and be at ease, without fear of harm.

Isaiah 32:18

KJV—My people shall dwell in a peaceable habitation, and in sure dwellings, and in quiet resting places.

AMP—My people shall dwell in a peaceable habitation, in safe dwellings, and in quiet resting places.

Moffatt—My people shall have homes of peace, resting in houses undisturbed.

NIV—My people will live in peaceful dwelling places, in secure homes, in undisturbed places of rest.

Isaiah 49:8-10

KJV—Thus saith the Lord, In an acceptable time have I heard thee, and in a day of salvation have I helped thee: and I will preserve thee, and give thee for a covenant of the people, to establish the earth, to cause to inherit the desolate heritages; That thou mayest say to the prisoners, Go forth; to them that are in darkness, Show yourselves.

They shall feed in the ways, and their pastures shall be in all high places. They shall not hunger nor thirst; neither shall the heat nor sun smite them: for he that hath mercy on them shall lead them, even by the springs of water shall he guide them.

AMP—Thus says the Lord, In an acceptable and favorable time I have heard and answered you, and in a day of salvation I have helped you; and I will preserve you and give you for a covenant to the people, to raise up and establish the land [from its present state of ruin], and to apportion and cause them to inherit the desolate [moral wastes of heathenism, their] heritages; Saying to those who are bound, Come forth; to those who are in spiritual darkness, Show yourselves—come into the light [of the Sun of righteousness]. They shall feed in all the ways [in which they go], and their pastures shall be [not in deserts, but] on all the bare [grass covered] hills. They shall not hunger or thirst, neither shall mirage mislead or scorching wind or sun smite them; for He Who has mercy on them will lead them, and by the springs of water will He guide them.

Isaiah 58:11

KJV—The Lord shall...satisfy thy soul in drought, and make fat thy bones: and thou shalt be like a watered garden, and like a spring of water, whose waters fail not.

AMP—The Lord shall satisfy you in drought and in dry places, and make strong your bones. And you shall be like a watered garden and like a spring of water, whose waters fail not.

Moffatt—The Eternal...will refresh you in dry places, and renew your strength, till you are like a watered garden, like an oasis with a steadfast spring.

NIV—The Lord will...satisfy your needs in a sun-scorched land and will strengthen your frame. You will be like a well-watered garden, like a spring whose waters never fail.

Jeremiah 32:21-22

KJV—[Thou] hast brought forth thy people Israel out of the land of Egypt with signs, and with wonders, and with a strong hand, and with a stretched out arm, and with great terror; And hast given them this land, which thou didst swear to their fathers to give them, a land flowing with milk and honey.

AMP—You brought forth Your people Israel out of the land of Egypt with signs and wonders, with a strong hand and outstretched arm, and with great terror; And You gave them this land which You swore to their fathers to give them, a land flowing with milk and honey.

Moffatt—From Egypt's land thou didst bring out thy people Israel with signal deeds of awe, by might and main, spreading terror around: thou gavest them this land which thou hadst sworn to their fathers to give them, a land abounding in milk and honey.

NIV—You brought your people Israel out of Egypt with signs and wonders, by a mighty hand and an outstretched arm and with great terror. You gave them this land you had sworn to give their forefathers, a land flowing with milk and honey.

Ezekiel 34:27-28

KJV—They shall be safe in their land, and shall know that I am the Lord, when I have broken the bands of their yoke, and delivered them.... And they shall no more be a prey to the heathen, neither shall the beast of the land devour them; but they shall dwell safely, and none shall make them afraid.

AMP—[My people] shall be secure in their land; and they shall be confident and know—understand and realize—that I am the Lord, when I have broken the bars of their yoke, and have delivered them.... And they shall no more be a prey to the nations, nor shall the beasts of the earth devour them; but they shall dwell safely, and none shall make them afraid [in the day of the Messiah's reign].

Moffatt—They shall live undisturbed in the land; they shall learn that I am the Eternal, when I break their yoke of slavery and rescue them.... They shall no longer be the prey of the nations, wild beasts shall not devour them, they shall live undisturbed, and none shall make them afraid.

NIV—The people will be secure in their land. They will know that I am the Lord, when I break the bars of their yoke and rescue them.... They will no longer be plundered by the nations, nor will wild animals devour them. They will live in safety, and no one will make them afraid.

Zephaniah 3:16-17

KJV—In that day it shall be said to Jerusalem, Fear thou not: and to Zion, Let not thine hands be slack. The Lord thy God in the midst of thee is mighty; he will save, he will rejoice over thee with joy; he will rest in his love, he will joy over thee with singing.

AMP—In that day it shall be said to Jerusalem, Fear not, O Zion. Let not your hands sink down or be slow and listless. The Lord your God is in the midst of you, a mighty One, a Savior—Who saves! He will rejoice over you with joy; He will rest [in silent satisfaction] and in His love He will be silent and make no mention [of past sins, or even recall them]; He will exult over you with singing.

Moffatt— [On that day shall Jerusalem be told, "Fear not, droop not your hands, O Sion."] The Eternal your God is in your midst, a warrior to the rescue; he thrills with joy over you, renews his love, exults with a festal song.

NIV—On that day they will say to Jerusalem, "Do not fear, O Zion; do not let your hands hang limp. The Lord your God is with you, he is mighty to save. He will take great delight in you, he will quiet you with his love, he will rejoice over you with singing."

235

*Enforcing
Jesus' Victory*

Protection Promises
WORD/SCRIPTURE INDEX

Angel(s)
Genesis 24:40; p. 20, 51, 160
Exodus 23:20-23; p. 160
Psalm 91; p. 1, 7, 13, 19, 23, 29, 37, 51-55, 57, 59-66
Psalm 103:20-22; p. 163
Acts 5:17-20; p. 164
Acts 12:5-11; p. 164
Acts 27:23-25; p. 165
Hebrews 1:13-14; p. 166

Authority (ies)
Luke 10:19; p. 42, 50-51, 54, 56, 59, 62, 65
Ephesians 1:15-23; p. 217
Ephesians 6:10-18; p. 197
Hebrews 2:14-15; p. 133,139
Revelation 12:10-11; p. 58

Battle
Deuteronomy 20:1, 3-4; p. 140
1 Samuel 17:47; p. 30, 51, 60, 62, 65
2 Samuel 22:40; p. 5, 35, 41, 51, 53, 59-65
2 Chronicles 20:15; p. 29-30, 41, 51, 53, 55, 59, 62-63
2 Chronicles 20:17; p. 29-30, 41, 51, 53, 55, 59, 62-63
Psalm 18:34; p. 5, 32, 35, 37, 41, 48, 51-54, 56-66
Psalm 18:39; p. 5, 32, 35, 37, 41, 48, 51-54, 56-66
Psalm 55:16, 18; p. 200
Ephesians 1:15-23; p. 217

Blood
Acts 5:24-29; p. 61
Ephesians 6:10-18; p. 197
Hebrews 2:14-15; p. 133,139
Hebrews 10:19-22; p. 56
Hebrews 13:12; p. 15, 51, 63
1 Peter 1:18-19; p. 57
Revelation 12:10-11; p. 58

Call (s), (ed), (eth)
Deuteronomy 30:19-20; p. 172
Psalm 3:4-5; p. 11
Psalm 18:3; p. 5, 32, 35, 37, 41, 48, 51-54, 56-66
Psalm 18:4-19; p. 12

Psalm 34:6; p. 41, 51-52, 56, 58, 60-62, 65
Psalm 50:15; p. 29, 51, 53, 65
Psalm 55:16-17; p. 14
Psalm 91:15; p. 1, 7, 13, 19, 24, 29, 37, 51-55, 57, 59-66
Psalm 145:18-20; p. 15
Isaiah 43:1-3; p. 202
Joel 2:32; p. 51, 53, 58, 62
Zechariah 13:9; p. 51, 56, 58, 63
Matthew 18:1-6; p. 177
John 10:3-5; p. 101
Acts 2:21; p. 46, 51, 54-55, 57-59, 63, 67
Romans 10:13-15; p. 225
Ephesians 1:15-23; p. 217

Child (ren)
Numbers 14:9; p. 15, 52-53, 55, 59, 63
Deuteronomy 4:40; p. 25, 41, 52-54, 57, 61-62, 66
Deuteronomy 12:28; p. 25, 47, 52, 56, 59-61, 64
Psalm 8:2; p. 48, 52, 54, 58-59, 61, 64
Psalm 37:25; p. 26, 52, 54-57, 59-62, 64-65
Psalm 103:13, 17-18; p. 173
Proverbs 4:3-4; p. 174
Proverbs 14:26; p. 27, 52, 55-56, 58-60, 65
Isaiah 9:6-7; p. 51
Isaiah 43:4-6; p. 175
Isaiah 49:25; p. 27, 48, 52-53, 55-56, 59, 61-63
Isaiah 59:19-21; p. 214
Matthew 1:23; p. 15, 39, 51-53, 55, 58, 65
Matthew 18:1-6; p. 177
Galatians 3:6-7, 27; p. 70
Hebrews 2:14-15; p. 133,139
1 John 4:3-4; p. 219

Confess (eth)
1 John 4:3-4; p. 219

Covenant
Genesis 6:13-14, 17-19; p. 65
Deuteronomy 4:31; p. 25, 41, 52-54, 57, 61-62, 66
Deuteronomy 7:9; p. 24-25, 52, 54-57, 60, 64, 66
1 Chronicles 16:15-22; p. 33

Psalm 25:10; p. 26, 52-53, 57-66
Psalm 103:13, 17-18; p. 173
Isaiah 49:8-10; p. 230
Isaiah 54:10; p. 38, 52, 55, 58, 61, 63, 65
Isaiah 59:19-21; p. 214
Luke 1:67-75; p. 53

Cover (ed)
Deuteronomy 33:12; p. 1, 47, 52, 60-61, 64
2 Kings 6:16-17; p. 162
Psalm 61:4; p. 5-6, 52, 54, 60, 64-66
Psalm 91; p. 1, 7, 13, 19, 24, 29, 37, 51-55, 57, 59-66
Psalm 109:29; p. 52-53, 57-59, 62, 64
Isaiah 49:8-10; p. 230
Isaiah 61:10; p. 52, 61-62
Ephesians 6:10-18; p. 197

Cry (ied)
Psalm 3:4-5; p. 11
Psalm 18:4-19; p. 12
Psalm 34:6; p. 41, 51-52, 56, 58, 60-62, 65
Psalm 34:15; p. 41, 51-52, 56, 58, 60-62, 65
Psalm 40:1-2; p. 98
Psalm 55:16-17; p. 14
Psalm 107:6-7; p. 24
Psalm 145:18-20; p. 15
Isaiah 19:20; p. 52-54, 58-59, 63, 65

Death
Deuteronomy 30:19-20; p. 172
Psalm 18:4-19; p. 12
Psalm 23; p. 29, 37, 52, 54-60, 63-64
Psalm 33:18-19; p. 37
Psalm 56:12-13; p. 37
Psalm 68:19-20; p. 38
Psalm 91:5-6; p. 141
Psalm 94:17-18; p. 39
Psalm 103:1-4; p. 40
Mark 16:16-18; p. 224
Hebrews 2:14-15; p. 133,139

Defense
Numbers 14:9; p. 15, 52-53, 55, 59, 63

Psalm 7:10; p. 4, 6, 33, 35, 38, 53-54, 56-57, 59-66
Psalm 31:1-3; p. 13
Psalm 59:9; p. 53-54, 56, 59-60, 64-66
Psalm 94:22; p. 8, 52-53, 59-61, 65
Mark 16:16-18; p. 224

Deliver (s), (ed), (er), (eth), (est), (ance)
Genesis 14:20; p. 40, 53-54, 56, 59
Exodus 14:13-14; p. 183
Deuteronomy 23:14; p. 32, 52-54, 57, 59
2 Samuel 22:2-3; p. 122
2 Kings 17:39; p. 31, 53-56
1 Chronicles 14:10; p. 31, 53, 59
2 Chronicles 20:17; p. 29-30, 41, 51, 53, 55, 59, 62-63
Ezra 8:31; p. 31, 53-54, 56, 59, 61
Psalm 6:4; p. 3, 16, 19, 51-58, 62-63, 65-66
Psalm 18:1-2; p. 123
Psalm 18:18-19; p. 228
Psalm 18:27-33; p. 93
Psalm 18:43; p. 5, 32, 35, 37, 41, 48, 51-54, 56-66
Psalm 25:20-21; p. 96
Psalm 27:11-12; p. 87
Psalm 31:1; p. 4, 6, 48, 53-57, 59-66
Psalm 32:7; p. 4, 53, 56, 59, 61, 63-65
Psalm 33:18-19; p. 37
Psalm 35:10; p. 33, 35, 53-54, 56, 58, 62-64, 66
Psalm 40:17; p. 52-59, 61, 64, 66
Psalm 41:1-2; p. 19
Psalm 50:15; p. 29, 51, 53, 65
Psalm 55:16, 18; p. 200
Psalm 56:12-13; p. 37
Psalm 68:19-20; p. 38
Psalm 71:2; p. 6, 8, 53-54, 60-62
Psalm 91:3-6; p. 158
Psalm 91:15; p. 1, 7, 13, 19, 24, 29, 37, 51-55, 57, 59-66
Psalm 107:1-3; p. 44
Psalm 107:6-7; p. 24
Psalm 108:5-6; p. 14
Psalm 109:29; p. 52-53, 57-59, 62, 64
Psalm 118:14-15; p. 67
Psalm 140:1, 4; p. 192

Proverbs 2:11-13; p. 80
Proverbs 11:8; p. 53, 60-61, 65
Proverbs 12:6; p. 53
Isaiah 19:20; p. 52-54, 58-59, 63, 65
Isaiah 43:1-3; p. 202
Isaiah 48:17; p. 53-54, 60, 63
Isaiah 49:25; p. 27, 48, 52-53, 55-56, 59, 61-63
Jeremiah 1:8; p. 17, 31, 53, 60, 63
Jeremiah 1:19; p. 17, 31, 53, 56, 59-60, 63
Jeremiah 15:20-21; p. 152
Jeremiah 42:11-12; p. 115
Ezekiel 34:27-28; p. 233
Daniel 3:17; p. 9, 53, 55, 59, 62-63
Daniel 6:25-27; p. 186
Joel 2:32; p. 51, 53, 58, 62
Matthew 10:17, 19-20; p. 204
Luke 1:67-75; p. 53
Acts 12:5-11; p. 164
Galatians 1:3-4; p. 116
Philippians 1:27-28; p. 155
Hebrews 2:14-15; p. 133,139
Hebrews 11:7; p. 54-55, 61, 63

Destroy (ed), (er), (ers)
Genesis 6:13-14, 17-19; p. 65
Deuteronomy 4:31; p. 25, 41, 52-54, 57, 61-62, 66
Psalm 17:1, 4-5; p. 83
Psalm 35:10; p. 33, 35, 53-54, 56, 58, 62-64, 66
Psalm 91:5-6; p. 141
Daniel 6:25-27; p. 186
Hebrews 2:14-15; p. 133,139

Direct (s)
Psalm 37:23-24; p. 88
Isaiah 48:17; p. 53-54, 60, 63

Enemy (ies)
Genesis 14:20; p. 40, 53-54, 56, 59
Genesis 22:17-18; p. 169
Exodus 23:20-23; p. 160
Leviticus 26:8; p. 40, 47, 54, 58, 60
Deuteronomy 6:17-19; p. 210
Deuteronomy 20:4; p. 12, 41, 51, 54-55, 62, 66

Deuteronomy 23:14; p. 32, 52-54, 57, 59
Deuteronomy 25:19; p. 47, 52, 54, 57, 60
Deuteronomy 28:1, 7; p. 29, 32
2 Kings 17:39; p. 31, 53-56
Ezra 8:31; p. 31, 53-54, 56, 59, 61
Psalm 8:2; p. 48, 52, 54, 58-59, 61, 64
Psalm 17:6, 8-9; p. 118
Psalm 18:3; p. 5, 32, 35, 37, 41, 48, 51-54, 56-66
Psalm 18:4-19; p. 12
Psalm 23:5; p. 29, 37, 52, 54-60, 63-64
Psalm 27:11-12; p. 87
Psalm 31:8; p. 4, 6, 48, 53-57, 59-66
Psalm 35:19; p. 33, 35, 53-56, 58, 62-64, 66
Psalm 41:1-2; p. 19
Psalm 41:11; p. 33, 53-54, 56-60, 65
Psalm 44:7; p. 33, 54, 61-62, 66
Psalm 61:3; p. 5-6, 52, 54, 60, 64-66
Psalm 68:1; p. 24, 33, 52-54, 59, 62
Psalm 89:21-22; p. 26
Psalm 107:1-3; p. 44
Psalm 110:1-2; p. 213
Psalm 119:98; p. 35, 54, 56, 60, 63-64
Psalm 138:7; p. 38, 54, 56-57, 59, 62, 65
Isaiah 41:10-14; p. 150
Isaiah 59:19-21; p. 214
Luke 1:67-75; p. 53
Luke 10:19; p. 42, 51, 54, 56, 59, 62, 65
Ephesians 6:10-18; p. 197
Hebrews 1:13-14; p. 166

Escape (s), (ed)
Psalm 68:19-20; p. 38
Psalm 71:2; p. 6, 8, 53-54, 60-62
Psalm 124:2-8; p. 222
Psalm 141:10; p. 9, 54, 61

Establish (ed)
Genesis 6:13-14, 17-19; p. 65
1 Chronicles 16:15-22; p. 33
Psalm 8:2; p. 48, 52, 54, 58-59, 61, 64
Psalm 37:23-24; p. 88

Psalm 40:1-2; p. 98
Psalm 89:21-22; p. 26
Psalm 107:6-7; p. 24
Psalm 112:1, 7-8; p. 159
Isaiah 9:6-7; p. 51
Isaiah 49:8-10; p. 230
Isaiah 54:14-15; p. 203
2 Thessalonians 3:3; p. 55, 57, 60

Fear (s), (ful)

Exodus 14:13-14; p. 183
Numbers 14:9; p. 15, 52-53, 55, 59, 63
Deuteronomy 1:29-30; p. 184
Deuteronomy 3:22; p. 30, 51, 55-56, 60, 64, 66
Deuteronomy 20:1, 3-4; p. 140
Deuteronomy 31:6, 8; p. 144
2 Kings 6:16-17; p. 162
2 Kings 17:39; p. 31, 53-56
2 Chronicles 20:15; p. 29-30, 41, 51, 53, 55, 59, 62-63
2 Chronicles 20:17; p. 29-30, 41, 51, 53, 55, 59, 62-63
Psalm 3:6; p. 6, 19, 33, 35, 51-52, 54-57, 59-62, 64-66
Psalm 23; p. 29, 37, 52, 54-60, 63-64
Psalm 27:1; p. 4, 16, 19, 53-59, 61-65
Psalm 27:3; p. 4, 16, 19, 53-59, 61-65
Psalm 31:19-20; p. 119
Psalm 33:18-19; p. 37
Psalm 56:3-4; p. 149
Psalm 91:5-6; p. 141
Psalm 103:13, 17-18; p. 173
Psalm 112:1, 7-8; p. 159
Psalm 118:6; p. 16, 53, 55, 61-62, 64, 66
Psalm 128:1-2; p. 100
Psalm 145:18-20; p. 15
Proverbs 1:33; p. 48, 52-53, 55-57, 59-62, 64-66
Proverbs 14:26; p. 27, 52, 55-56, 58-60, 65
Isaiah 35:3-4; p. 142
Isaiah 41:10-14; p. 150
Isaiah 43:1-3; p. 202
Isaiah 43:4-6; p. 175
Isaiah 44:8; p. 2, 55, 59, 61
Isaiah 51:12; p. 17, 55
Isaiah 54:14-15; p. 203
Jeremiah 42:11-12; p. 115
Ezekiel 2:6; p. 18, 55, 63

Daniel 6:25-27; p. 186
Daniel 10:18-19; p. 22
Zephaniah 3:16-17; p. 234
Matthew 10:28-31; p. 136
Mark 4:37-41; p. 109
Mark 5:36; p. 11, 55, 57-58, 63
Luke 1:67-75; p. 53
John 14:23, 27; p. 138
Acts 27:23-25; p. 165
Philippians 1:27-28; p. 155
2 Timothy 1:7; p. 10, 14, 55, 59
Hebrews 2:14-15; p. 133,139
Hebrews 11:7; p. 54-55, 61, 63
1 Peter 3:14; p. 55, 65-66

Generation

Deuteronomy 7:9; p. 24-25, 52, 54-57, 60, 64, 66
1 Chronicles 16:15-22; p. 33

Hand (of the Lord)

Deuteronomy 7:8; p. 24-25, 52, 54-57, 60, 64, 66
Ezra 8:31; p. 31, 53-54, 56, 59, 61
Psalm 17:7; p. 3, 53-54, 56-58, 60, 62-66
Psalm 18:35; p. 5, 32, 35, 37, 41, 48, 51-54, 56-66
Psalm 31:3-6; p. 97
Psalm 37:23-24; p. 88
Psalm 73:20, 23-24; p. 89
Psalm 89:21-22; p. 26
Psalm 95:7; p. 56
Psalm 108:5-6; p. 14
Psalm 138:7; p. 38, 54, 56-57, 59, 62, 65
Isaiah 41:10-14; p. 150
Isaiah 59:1; p. 42, 52, 54, 56, 60, 62-63
Jeremiah 32:21-22; p. 232
Zechariah 2:8-9; p. 193
Mark 10:13-16; p. 178
Ephesians 1:15-23; p. 217
Hebrews 1:13-14; p. 166

Harm

1 Chronicles 16:15-22; p. 33
Psalm 23; p. 29, 37, 52, 54-60, 63-64
Psalm 121:1-8; p. 89
Proverbs 1:33; p. 48, 52-53, 55-57, 59-62, 64-66
Mark 16:16-18; p. 224
Luke 10:19; p. 42, 51, 54, 56, 59, 62, 65

John 16:33; p. 2, 52, 56-60, 65-66
Acts 18:9-10; p. 154

Hear (d), (s), (eth)

Genesis 22:17-18; p. 169
Deuteronomy 12:28; p. 25, 47, 52, 56, 59-61, 64
Psalm 3:4-5; p. 11
Psalm 18:4-19; p. 12
Psalm 20:1; p. 45, 56-57, 59, 65
Psalm 34:6; p. 41, 51-52, 56, 58, 60-62, 65
Psalm 40:1-2; p. 98
Psalm 55:16-17; p. 14
Psalm 103:13, 17-18; p. 173
Psalm 145:18-20; p. 15
Isaiah 30:21; p. 52, 56, 58, 63-64, 66
Isaiah 49:8-10; p. 230
Isaiah 59:1; p. 42, 52, 54, 56, 60, 62-63
Zechariah 13:9; p. 51, 56, 58, 63
Luke 6:47-48; p. 76, 82
John 10:3-5; p. 101
John 16:13-15; p. 60
Acts 4:1-2, 18-21; p. 60
Romans 10:13-15; p. 225
Philippians 1:27-28; p. 155
1 John 4:3-4; p. 219

Hide (s), (ing)

Psalm 17:6, 8-9; p. 118
Psalm 27:5; p. 4, 16, 19, 53-59, 61-65
Psalm 31:19-20; p. 119
Psalm 32:7; p. 4, 53, 56, 59, 61, 63-65
Psalm 64:1-2; p. 121
Psalm 119:114; p. 35, 54, 56, 60, 63-64
Proverbs 2:6-8; p. 79

Keep (s)

Genesis 6:13-14, 17-19; p. 65
Genesis 28:15; p. 56, 66
Exodus 14:13-14; p. 183
Exodus 23:20-23; p. 160
Leviticus 25:18-19; p. 226
Deuteronomy 4:40; p. 25, 41, 52-54, 57, 61-62, 66
Deuteronomy 6:17-19; p. 210
Deuteronomy 7:9; p. 24-25, 52, 54-57, 60, 64, 66
1 Kings 11:38; p. 57
Psalm 17:1, 4-5; p. 83

Psalm 25:10; p. 26, 52-53, 57-66

Psalm 25:20-21; p. 96

Psalm 27:5; p. 4, 16, 19, 53-59, 61-65

Psalm 31:19-20; p. 119

Psalm 31:23-24; p. 98

Psalm 33:18-19; p. 37

Psalm 40:11; p. 52-59, 61, 64, 66

Psalm 41:1-2; p. 19

Psalm 66:8-9; p. 38

Psalm 91; p. 1, 7, 13, 19, 24, 29, 37, 51-55, 57, 59-66

Psalm 103:13, 17-18; p. 173

Psalm 121:1-8; p. 89

Proverbs 2:11-13; p. 80

Proverbs 4:3-4; p. 174

Proverbs 4:4-6; p. 81

Isaiah 26:1-2; p. 130

Mark 5:36; p. 11, 55, 57-58, 63

John 16:33; p. 2, 52, 56-60, 65-66

John 17:1, 11, 14-15; p. 27

Acts 18:9-10; p. 154

Acts 27:23-25; p. 165

2 Thessalonians 3:3; p. 55, 57, 60

Life

Genesis 6:13-14, 17-19; p. 65

Deuteronomy 5:16; p. 57, 59, 61

Deuteronomy 30:19-20; p. 172

Psalm 6:4; p. 3, 16, 19, 51-58, 62-63, 65-66

Psalm 23; p. 29, 37, 52, 54-60, 63-64

Psalm 25:20-21; p. 96

Psalm 27:1; p. 4, 16, 19, 53-59, 61-65

Psalm 31:3-6; p. 97

Psalm 37:23-24; p. 88

Psalm 41:1-2; p. 19

Psalm 55:16, 18; p. 200

Psalm 56:12-13; p. 37

Psalm 66:8-9; p. 38

Psalm 91:16; p. 1, 7, 13, 19, 24, 29, 37, 51-55, 57, 59-66

Psalm 103:1-4; p. 40

Psalm 109:30-31; p. 20

Psalm 121:1-8; p. 89

Psalm 138:7; p. 38, 54, 56-57, 59, 62, 65

Proverbs 3:21-24; p. 108

Proverbs 4:20-24; p. 103

Luke 1:67-75; p. 53

John 3:16-17; p. 55

Philippians 1:27-28; p. 155

Name (of the Lord)

Exodus 23:20-23; p. 160

Psalm 20:1; p. 45, 56-57, 59, 65

Psalm 20:7-8; p. 221

Psalm 23; p. 29, 37, 52, 54-60, 63-64

Psalm 31:3; p. 4, 6, 48, 53-57, 59-66

Psalm 89:21-24; p. 222

Psalm 91; p. 1, 7, 13, 19, 24, 29, 37, 51-55, 57, 59-66

Psalm 103:1-4; p. 40

Psalm 124:2-8; p. 222

Proverbs 18:10; p. 1, 57, 61, 64-66

Isaiah 9:6-7; p. 51

Isaiah 43:1-3; p. 202

Joel 2:32; p. 51, 53, 58, 62

Zechariah 13:9; p. 51, 56, 58, 63

Matthew 1:23; p. 15, 39, 51-53, 55, 58, 65

Matthew 18:1-6; p. 177

Matthew 24:4-6; p. 137

Mark 16:16-18; p. 224

John 17:1, 11, 14-15; p. 27

Acts 2:21; p. 46, 51, 54-55, 57-59, 63, 67

Acts 3:12, 16; p. 225

Acts 4:1-2, 18-21; p. 60

Ephesians 1:15-23; p. 217

Oppress (ion), (ors)

1 Chronicles 16:15-22; p. 33

Psalm 12:5; p. 1, 58-59, 61-63

Psalm 17:6, 8-9; p. 118

Psalm 27:11-12; p. 87

Psalm 89:21-22; p. 26

Isaiah 19:20; p. 52-54, 58-59, 63, 65

Isaiah 41:10-14; p. 150

Isaiah 54:14-15; p. 203

Path (s)

Psalm 17:1, 4-5; p. 83

Psalm 18:27-33; p. 93

Psalm 18:36; p. 5, 32, 35, 37, 41, 48, 51-54, 56-66

Psalm 23; p. 29, 37, 52, 54-60, 63-64

Psalm 25:4-5; p. 95

Psalm 25:10; p. 26, 52-53, 57-66

Psalm 27:11-12; p. 87

Proverbs 2:6-8; p. 79

Proverbs 2:11-13; p. 80

Isaiah 30:21; p. 52, 56, 58, 63-64, 66

Jeremiah 31:9; p. 58

Peace (able)

Exodus 14:13-14; p. 183

Leviticus 26:6; p. 40, 47, 54, 58, 60

Psalm 4:8; p. 1, 5, 24, 34, 52-53, 57-66

Psalm 55:16, 18; p. 200

Isaiah 9:6-7; p. 51

Isaiah 32:18; p. 48, 51, 56, 58, 60-62

Isaiah 54:10; p. 38, 52, 55, 58, 61, 63, 65

Isaiah 54:17; p. 38, 52, 55, 58, 61, 63, 65

Isaiah 58:8; p. 49, 58-61, 65

Daniel 10:18-19; p. 22

Mark 4:37-41; p. 109

John 14:23, 27; p. 138

John 16:33; p. 2, 52, 56-60, 65-66

Acts 18:9-10; p. 154

Romans 10:13-15; p. 225

Ephesians 6:10-18; p. 197

Poor

Psalm 12:5; p. 1, 58-59, 61-63

Psalm 34:6; p. 41, 51-52, 56, 58, 60-62, 65

Psalm 35:10; p. 33, 35, 53-54, 56, 58, 62-64, 66

Psalm 40:17; p. 52-59, 61, 64, 66

Psalm 41:1-2; p. 19

Psalm 109:30-31; p. 20

Mark 16:16-18; p. 224

Power

2 Samuel 22:33-34; p. 194

2 Chronicles 14:11; p. 53, 59

Job 36:5; p. 59, 64, 66

Psalm 91; p. 1, 7, 13, 19, 24, 29, 37, 51-55, 57, 59-66

Isaiah 40:28-29; p. 21

Isaiah 44:8; p. 2, 55, 59, 61

Isaiah 58:8; p. 49, 58-61, 65

Jeremiah 42:11-12; p. 115

Daniel 6:25-27; p. 186

Luke 10:19; p. 42, 51, 54, 56, 59, 62, 65

John 17:1, 11, 14-15; p. 27

Acts 3:12, 16; p. 225

Ephesians 1:15-23; p. 217

Ephesians 6:10-18; p. 197

2 Timothy 1:7; p. 10, 14, 55, 59

Revelation 12:10-11; p. 58

Powerless

2 Chronicles 14:11; p. 53, 59

Hebrews 2:14-15; p. 133,139

Praise (d)

Genesis 14:20; p. 40, 53-54, 56, 59

Psalm 8:2; p. 48, 52, 54, 58-59, 61, 64

Psalm 18:3; p. 5, 32, 35, 37, 41, 48, 51-54, 56-66

Psalm 56:3-4; p. 149

Psalm 59:9; p. 53-54, 56, 59-60, 64-66

Psalm 66:8-9; p. 38

Psalm 68:19-20; p. 38

Psalm 103:1-4; p. 40

Psalm 109:30-31; p. 20

Preserve (d), (s), (eth)

Psalm 25:20-21; p. 96

Psalm 31:23-24; p. 98

Psalm 32:7; p. 4, 53, 56, 59, 61, 63-65

Psalm 37:28; p. 26, 52, 54-57, 59-62, 64-65

Psalm 40:11; p. 52-59, 61, 64, 66

Psalm 41:1-2; p. 19

Psalm 66:8-9; p. 38

Psalm 91; p. 1, 7, 13, 19, 24, 29, 37, 51-55, 57, 59-66

Psalm 121:1-8; p. 89

Psalm 138:7; p. 38, 54, 56-57, 59, 62, 65

Psalm 140:1, 4; p. 192

Psalm 145:18-20; p. 15

Proverbs 2:6-8; p. 79

Proverbs 2:11-13; p. 80

Proverbs 3:21-24; p. 108

Proverbs 4:4-6; p. 81

Isaiah 49:8-10; p. 230

Protect (s), (ed), (or), (tion)

Numbers 14:9; p. 15, 52-53, 55, 59, 63

Deuteronomy 23:14; p. 32, 52-54, 57, 59

Ezra 8:31; p. 31, 53-54, 56, 59, 61

Psalm 125; p. 1, 58-59, 61-63

Psalm 20:1; p. 45, 56-57, 59, 65

Psalm 23; p. 29, 37, 52, 54-60, 63-64

Psalm 25:20-21; p. 96

Psalm 27:1; p. 4, 16, 19, 53-59, 61-65

Psalm 31:1-3; p. 123

Psalm 32:7; p. 4, 53, 56, 59, 61, 63-65

Psalm 37:28; p. 26, 52, 54-57, 59-62, 64-65

Psalm 40:11; p. 52-59, 61, 64, 66

Psalm 41:1-2; p. 19

Psalm 59:9; p. 53-54, 56, 59-60, 64-66

Psalm 91:3-6; p. 158

Psalm 94:22; p. 8, 52-53, 59-61, 65

Psalm 121:1-8; p. 89

Psalm 140:1, 4; p. 192

Proverbs 2:6-8; p. 79

Proverbs 2:11-13; p. 80

Proverbs 4:4-6; p. 81

John 17:1, 11, 14-15; p. 27

2 Thessalonians 3:3; p. 55, 57, 60

Redeem (ed), (er), (eth)

Deuteronomy 7:8; p. 24-25, 52, 54-57, 60, 64, 66

Psalm 31:3-6; p. 97

Psalm 55:16, 18; p. 200

Psalm 103:1-4; p. 40

Psalm 107:1-3; p. 44

Isaiah 41:10-14; p. 150

Isaiah 43:1-3; p. 202

Isaiah 48:17; p. 53-54, 60, 63

Isaiah 59:19-21; p. 214

Jeremiah 15:20-21; p. 152

Luke 1:67-75; p. 53

1 Peter 1:18-19; p. 57

Refuge

Deuteronomy 33:26-27; p. 113

2 Samuel 22:2-3; p. 122

Psalm 17:7; p. 3, 53-54, 56-58, 60, 62-66

Psalm 18:1-2; p. 123

Psalm 18:27-33; p. 93

Psalm 25:20-21; p. 96

Psalm 31:1; p. 4, 6, 48, 53-57, 59-66

Psalm 31:3-6; p. 97

Psalm 31:19-20; p. 119

Psalm 46:1; p. 6, 19, 60, 64-65

Psalm 57:1; p. 4, 33, 60, 62-64, 66

Psalm 61:3; p. 5-6, 52, 54, 60, 64-66

Psalm 61:4; p. 5-6, 52, 54, 60, 64-66

Psalm 62:6-8; p. 125

Psalm 71:7; p. 6, 8, 53-54, 60-62

Psalm 91:2; p. 1, 7, 13, 19, 24, 29, 37, 51-55, 57, 59-66

Psalm 91:3-6; p. 158

Psalm 94:22; p. 8, 52-53, 59-61, 65

Psalm 119:114; p. 35, 54, 56, 60, 63-64

Proverbs 14:26; p. 27, 52, 55-56, 58-60, 65

Proverbs 30:5; p. 36, 58, 60-64

Rest (ing)

Exodus 33:14; p. 47, 60-61

Leviticus 26:6; p. 40, 47, 54, 58, 60

Deuteronomy 25:19; p. 47, 52, 54, 57, 60

Deuteronomy 33:12; p. 1, 47, 52, 60-61, 64

Isaiah 32:18; p. 48, 51, 56, 58, 60-62

Zephaniah 3:16-17; p. 234

Restore (eth), (ation)

Psalm 23; p. 29, 37, 52, 54-60, 63-64

Isaiah 58:8; p. 49, 58-61, 65

Righteous (ness)

Genesis 15:6; p. 56, 60

Psalm 31:1; p. 4, 6, 48, 53-57, 59-66

Psalm 34:15; p. 41, 51-52, 56, 58, 60-62, 65

Psalm 37:25; p. 26, 52, 54-57, 59-62, 64-65

Psalm 71:2; p. 6, 8, 53-54, 60-62

Psalm 103:13, 17-18; p. 173

Psalm 118:14-15; p. 67

Proverbs 2:6-8; p. 79

Proverbs 11:8; p. 53, 60-61, 65

Proverbs 18:10; p. 1, 57, 61, 64-66

Proverbs 30:5; p. 36, 58, 60-64

Isaiah 9:6-7; p. 51

Isaiah 26:1-2; p. 130

Isaiah 41:10-14; p. 150

Isaiah 54:14-15; p. 203

Isaiah 54:17; p. 38, 52, 55, 58, 61, 63, 65

Isaiah 58:8; p. 49, 58-61, 65
Isaiah 61:10; p. 52, 61-62
Luke 1:67-75; p. 53
2 Corinthians 5:18, 21; p. 70
Galatians 3:6-7, 27; p. 70
Ephesians 4:22-24; p. 71
Ephesians 6:10-18; p. 197
Hebrews 11:7; p. 54-55, 61, 63

Rock
2 Samuel 22:2-3; p. 122
Psalm 18:1-2; p. 123
Psalm 18:27-33; p. 93
Psalm 27:5; p. 4, 16, 19, 53-59, 61-65
Psalm 31:3; p. 4, 6, 48, 53-57, 59-66
Psalm 40:1-2; p. 98
Psalm 62:6-8; p. 125
Psalm 94:22; p. 8, 52-53, 59-61, 65
Isaiah 44:8; p. 2, 55, 59, 61
Luke 6:47-48; p. 76, 82

Safe (ty), (ly), (guard)
Exodus 33:14; p. 47, 60-61
Leviticus 25:18-19; p. 226
Deuteronomy 33:12; p. 1, 47, 52, 60-61, 64
Ezra 8:31; p. 31, 53-54, 56, 59, 61
Psalm 4:8; p. 1, 5, 24, 34, 52-53, 57-66
Psalm 12:5; p. 1, 58-59, 61-63
Psalm 27:5; p. 4, 16, 19, 53-59, 61-65
Psalm 31:3-6; p. 97
Psalm 31:19-20; p. 119
Psalm 32:7; p. 4, 53, 56, 59, 61, 63-65
Psalm 62:6-8; p. 125
Psalm 66:8-9; p. 38
Psalm 91:2; p. 1, 7, 13, 19, 24, 29, 37, 51-55, 57, 59-66
Psalm 94:22; p. 8, 52-53, 59-61, 65
Psalm 141:10; p. 9, 54, 61
Proverbs 1:33; p. 48, 52-53, 55-57, 59-62, 64-66
Proverbs 2:6-8; p. 79
Proverbs 3:21-24; p. 108
Proverbs 11:8; p. 53, 60-61, 65
Proverbs 18:10; p. 1, 57, 61, 64-66
Proverbs 21:30-31; p. 114
Isaiah 26:1-2; p. 130

Isaiah 32:18; p. 48, 51, 56, 58, 60-62
Isaiah 49:25; p. 27, 48, 52-53, 55-56, 59, 61-63
Jeremiah 42:11-12; p. 115
Ezekiel 34:27-28; p. 233
John 3:16-17; p. 55

Salvation
Exodus 14:13-14; p. 183
2 Samuel 22:2-3; p. 122
2 Chronicles 20:17; p. 29-30, 41, 51, 53, 55, 59, 62-63
Psalm 12:5; p. 1, 58-59, 61-63
Psalm 18:1-2; p. 123
Psalm 18:35; p. 5, 32, 35, 37, 41, 48, 51-54, 56-66
Psalm 25:4-5; p. 95
Psalm 27:1; p. 4, 16, 19, 53-59, 61-65
Psalm 62:6-8; p. 125
Psalm 68:19-20; p. 38
Psalm 91:16; p. 1, 7, 13, 19, 24, 29, 37, 51-55, 57, 59-66
Psalm 109:29; p. 52-53, 57-59, 62, 64
Psalm 118:14-15; p. 67
Proverbs 30:5; p. 36, 58, 60-64
Isaiah 26:1-2; p. 130
Isaiah 49:8-10; p. 230
Isaiah 61:10; p. 52, 61-62
Luke 1:67-75; p. 53
John 3:16-17; p. 55
Ephesians 6:17-18; p. 105
Philippians 1:27-28; p. 155
Hebrews 1:13-14; p. 166
Revelation 12:10-11; p. 58

Save (s), (ed), (est), (ing)
Deuteronomy 20:1, 3-4; p. 140
1 Samuel 17:47; p. 30, 51, 60, 62, 65
2 Samuel 22:2-3; p. 122
Psalm 6:4; p. 3, 16, 19, 51-58, 62-63, 65-66
Psalm 7:10; p. 4, 6, 33, 35, 38, 53-54, 56-57, 59-66
Psalm 17:7; p. 3, 53-54, 56-58, 60, 62-66
Psalm 18:1-2; p. 123
Psalm 18:3; p. 5, 32, 35, 37, 41, 48, 51-54, 56-66
Psalm 18:27-33; p. 93
Psalm 31:3-6; p. 97
Psalm 34:6; p. 41, 51-52, 56, 58, 60-62, 65

Psalm 44:7; p. 33, 54, 61-62, 66
Psalm 55:16-17; p. 14
Psalm 56:12-13; p. 37
Psalm 57:3; p. 4, 33, 60, 62-64, 66
Psalm 68:19-20; p. 38
Psalm 71:2; p. 6, 8, 53-54, 60-62
Psalm 91:16; p. 1, 7, 13, 19, 24, 29, 37, 51-55, 57, 59-66
Psalm 103:1-4; p. 40
Psalm 107:6-7; p. 24
Psalm 108:5-6; p. 14
Psalm 109:29; p. 52-53, 57-59, 62, 64
Psalm 109:30-31; p. 20
Psalm 138:7; p. 38, 54, 56-57, 59, 62, 65
Psalm 140:1, 4; p. 192
Psalm 145:18-20; p. 15
Proverbs 2:11-13; p. 80
Proverbs 21:30-31; p. 114
Proverbs 30:5; p. 36, 58, 60-64
Isaiah 35:3-4; p. 142
Isaiah 49:25; p. 27, 48, 52-53, 55-56, 59, 61-63
Isaiah 59:1; p. 42, 52, 54, 56, 60, 62-63
Jeremiah 15:20-21; p. 152
Jeremiah 42:11-12; p. 115
Daniel 3:17; p. 9, 53, 55, 59, 62-63
Joel 2:32; p. 51, 53, 58, 62
Zephaniah 3:16-17; p. 234
Mark 16:16-18; p. 224
Luke 1:67-75; p. 53
Acts 2:21; p. 46, 51, 54-55, 57-59, 63, 67
Romans 10:13-15; p. 225
Galatians 1:3-4; p. 116
Ephesians 6:10-18; p. 197
Philippians 1:27-28; p. 155
Hebrews 11:7; p. 54-55, 61, 63

Say (s), (ing), (ings), (id), (ith)
Numbers 14:9; p. 15, 52-53, 55, 59, 63
Joshua 1:5; p. 14, 63, 65
1 Chronicles 16:15-22; p. 33
2 Chronicles 20:15; p. 29-30, 41, 51, 53, 55, 59, 62-63
Psalm 12:5; p. 1, 58-59, 61-63
Psalm 35:10; p. 33, 35, 53-54, 56, 58, 62-64, 66

Psalm 91:2; p. 1, 7, 13, 19, 24, 29, 37, 51-55, 57, 59-66
Psalm 107:1-3; p. 44
Psalm 110:1-2; p. 213
Proverbs 4:3-4; p. 174
Proverbs 4:4-6; p. 81
Proverbs 4:20-24; p. 103
Isaiah 30:21; p. 52, 56, 58, 63-64, 66
Isaiah 35:3-4; p. 142
Isaiah 41:10-14; p. 150
Isaiah 45:1-2; p. 90
Isaiah 48:17; p. 53-54, 60, 63
Isaiah 49:8-10; p. 230
Isaiah 49:25; p. 27, 48, 52-53, 55-56, 59, 61-63
Isaiah 54:10; p. 38, 52, 55, 58, 61, 63, 65
Isaiah 54:17; p. 38, 52, 55, 58, 61, 63, 65
Isaiah 59:19-21; p. 214
Jeremiah 1:19; p. 17, 31, 53, 56, 59-60, 63
Jeremiah 15:20-21; p. 152
Jeremiah 42:11-12; p. 115
Ezekiel 2:6; p. 18, 55, 63
Daniel 10:18-19; p. 22
Zephaniah 3:16-17; p. 234
Zechariah 2:8-9; p. 193
Zechariah 13:9; p. 51, 56, 58, 63
Matthew 10:17, 19-20; p. 204
Matthew 10:18-20; p. 59
Matthew 28:18, 20; p. 146
Mark 11:22-24; p. 104
Luke 6:47-48; p. 76, 82
Hebrews 13:5; p. 15, 51, 63

Shade
Psalm 121:1-8; p. 89
Mark 16:16-18; p. 224

Shadow
Numbers 14:9; p. 15, 52-53, 55, 59, 63
Psalm 17:6, 8-9; p. 118
Psalm 23; p. 29, 37, 52, 54-60, 63-64
Psalm 57:1; p. 4, 33, 60, 62-64, 66
Psalm 91; p. 1, 7, 13, 19, 24, 29, 37, 51-55, 57, 59-66
Mark 16:16-18; p. 224

Shelter
2 Samuel 22:2-3; p. 122
Psalm 18:27-33; p. 93

Psalm 25:20-21; p. 96
Psalm 27:5; p. 4, 16, 19, 53-59, 61-65
Psalm 31:1; p. 4, 6, 48, 53-57, 59-66
Psalm 31:19-20; p. 119
Psalm 32:7; p. 4, 53, 56, 59, 61, 63-65
Psalm 46:1; p. 6, 19, 60, 64-65
Psalm 57:1; p. 4, 33, 60, 62-64, 66
Psalm 61:3; p. 5-6, 52, 54, 60, 64-66
Psalm 61:4; p. 5-6, 52, 54, 60, 64-66
Psalm 91:3-6; p. 158
Psalm 119:114; p. 35, 54, 56, 60, 63-64
Psalm 121:1-8; p. 89
Proverbs 30:5; p. 36, 58, 60-64
Mark 16:16-18; p. 224

Shield
Deuteronomy 33:12; p. 1, 47, 52, 60-61, 64
2 Samuel 22:2-3; p. 122
Psalm 3:3; p. 6, 19, 33, 35, 51-52, 54-57, 59-62, 64-66
Psalm 7:10; p. 4, 6, 33, 35, 38, 53-54, 56-57, 59-66
Psalm 18:1-2; p. 123
Psalm 18:27-33; p. 93
Psalm 18:35; p. 5, 32, 35, 37, 41, 48, 51-54, 56-66
Psalm 23; p. 29, 37, 52, 54-60, 63-64
Psalm 91:3-6; p. 158
Psalm 109:29; p. 52-53, 57-59, 62, 64
Psalm 119:114; p. 35, 54, 56, 60, 63-64
Proverbs 2:6-8; p. 79
Proverbs 30:5; p. 36, 58, 60-64
Ephesians 6:10-18; p. 197

Sleep
Psalm 3:3-5; p. 11
Psalm 4:8; p. 1, 5, 24, 34, 52-53, 57-66
Psalm 121:1-8; p. 89
Proverbs 3:21-24; p. 108

Steps
Psalm 17:1, 4-5; p. 83

Psalm 18:36; p. 5, 32, 35, 37, 41, 48, 51-54, 56-66
Psalm 37:23-24; p. 88
Psalm 40:1-2; p. 98
Psalm 140:1, 4; p. 192

Strength (en)
Deuteronomy 7:8; p. 24-25, 52, 54-57, 60, 64, 66
2 Samuel 22:2-3; p. 122
2 Samuel 22:33-34; p. 194
2 Samuel 22:40; p. 5, 35, 41, 51, 53, 59-65
Job 36:5; p. 59, 64, 66
Psalm 8:2; p. 48, 52, 54, 58-59, 61, 64
Psalm 18:1-2; p. 123
Psalm 18:27-33; p. 93
Psalm 18:39; p. 5, 32, 35, 37, 41, 48, 51-54, 56-66
Psalm 24:8; p. 64
Psalm 27:1; p. 4, 16, 19, 53-59, 61-65
Psalm 31:3-6; p. 97
Psalm 31:23-24; p. 98
Psalm 37:39; p. 26, 52, 54-57, 59-62, 64-65
Psalm 46:1; p. 6, 19, 60, 64-65
Psalm 59:9; p. 53-54, 56, 59-60, 64-66
Psalm 62:6-8; p. 125
Psalm 89:21-22; p. 26
Psalm 103:20-22; p. 163
Psalm 109:29; p. 52-53, 57-59, 62, 64
Psalm 110:1-2; p. 213
Psalm 118:14-15; p. 67
Proverbs 18:10; p. 1, 57, 61, 64-66
Isaiah 35:3-4; p. 142
Isaiah 40:28-29; p. 21
Isaiah 41:10-14; p. 150
Isaiah 58:11; p. 49, 58-61, 65
Daniel 10:18-19; p. 22
Mark 16:16-18; p. 224
Luke 10:19; p. 42, 51, 54, 56, 59, 62, 65
Ephesians 1:15-23; p. 217
Ephesians 6:10-18; p. 197
Revelation 12:10-11, p. 58

Stronghold
2 Samuel 22:2-3; p. 122
2 Samuel 22:33-34; p. 194
Psalm 18:1-2; p. 123
Psalm 31:3-6; p. 97
Psalm 37:39; p. 26, 52, 54-57, 59-62, 64-65

Psalm 46:1; p. 6, 19, 60, 64–65
Psalm 59:9; p. 53–54, 56, 59–60, 64–66
Mark 16:16–18; p. 224
2 Corinthians 10:3–5; p. 216

Surround (s), (ing)
Psalm 17:6, 8–9; p. 118
Psalm 32:7; p. 4, 53, 56, 59, 61, 63–65
Psalm 32:10; p. 4, 51, 53, 56, 58–59, 61, 63–65
Psalm 125:1–2; p. 99

Terror
Deuteronomy 31:6, 8; p. 144
Joshua 1:9; p. 14, 63, 65
Psalm 91:5–6; p. 141
Isaiah 41:10–14; p. 150
Isaiah 54:14–15; p. 203
1 Peter 3:14; p. 55, 65–66

Tower
2 Samuel 22:2–3; p. 122
Psalm 18:1–2; p. 123
Psalm 59:9; p. 53–54, 56, 59–60, 64–66
Psalm 61:3; p. 5–6, 52, 54, 60, 64–66
Psalm 62:6–8; p. 125
Psalm 94:22; p. 8, 52–53, 59–61, 65
Proverbs 18:10; p. 1, 57, 61, 64–66

Trouble (s), (ed)
Psalm 18:27–33; p. 93
Psalm 20:1; p. 45, 56–57, 59, 65
Psalm 27:5; p. 4, 16, 19, 53–59, 61–65
Psalm 32:7; p. 4, 53, 56, 59, 61, 63–65

Psalm 34:6; p. 41, 51–52, 56, 58, 60–62, 65
Psalm 37:39; p. 26, 52, 54–57, 59–62, 64–65
Psalm 41:1–2; p. 19
Psalm 46:1; p. 6, 19, 60, 64–65
Psalm 46:2–3; p. 157
Psalm 50:15; p. 29, 51, 53, 65
Psalm 91:15; p. 1, 7, 13, 19, 24, 29, 37, 51–55, 57, 59–66
Psalm 107:6–7; p. 24
Psalm 138:7; p. 38, 54, 56–57, 59, 62, 65
Proverbs 11:8; p. 53, 60–61, 65
Matthew 24:4–6; p. 137
John 14:23, 27; p. 138
John 16:33; p. 2, 52, 56–60, 65–66
1 Peter 3:14; p. 55, 65–66

Victory (ious)
Deuteronomy 20:4; p. 12, 41, 51, 54–55, 62, 66
Psalm 18:35; p. 5, 32, 35, 37, 41, 48, 51–54, 56–66
Psalm 44:7; p. 33, 54, 61–62, 66
Psalm 108:13; p. 41, 53, 56, 62, 66
Psalm 118:14–15; p. 67
Proverbs 2:6–8; p. 79
Proverbs 21:30–31; p. 114
Isaiah 41:10–14; p. 150
John 16:33; p. 2, 52, 56–60, 65–66
1 John 5:4; p. 44, 66
Revelation 12:10–11; p. 58

Voice
Genesis 22:17–18; p. 169
Exodus 23:20–23; p. 160
Deuteronomy 28:1, 7; p. 29, 32

Deuteronomy 30:19–20; p. 172
Psalm 3:4–5; p. 11
Psalm 18:4–19; p. 12
Psalm 55:16–17; p. 14
Psalm 66:8–9; p. 38
Psalm 103:20–22; p. 163
Psalm 118:14–15; p. 67
Isaiah 30:21; p. 52, 56, 58, 63–64, 66
John 10:3–5; p. 101

Wait (ed)
Psalm 25:4–5; p. 95
Psalm 25:20–21; p. 96
Psalm 31:23–24; p. 98
Psalm 33:18–19; p. 37
Psalm 40:1–2; p. 98
Psalm 59:9; p. 53–54, 56, 59–60, 64–66

Wings
Psalm 17:6, 8–9; p. 118
Psalm 31:19–20; p. 119
Psalm 57:1; p. 4, 33, 60, 62–64, 66
Psalm 61:4; p. 5–6, 52, 54, 60, 64–66
Psalm 91:3–6; p. 158

Wisdom
Job 36:5; p. 59, 64, 66
Proverbs 1:33; p. 48, 52–53, 55–57, 59–62, 64–66
Proverbs 2:6–8; p. 79
Proverbs 2:11–13; p. 80
Proverbs 3:21–24; p. 108
Proverbs 4:4–6; p. 81
Proverbs 21:30–31; p. 114
Luke 21:15, 18; p. 105
Ephesians 1:15–23; p. 217

Prayer for Salvation
and Baptism in the Holy Spirit

Heavenly Father, I come to You in the Name of Jesus. Your Word says, "*Whosoever shall call on the name of the Lord shall be saved*" (Acts 2:21). I am calling on You. I pray and ask Jesus to come into my heart and be Lord over my life, according to Romans 10:9—"*If thou shalt confess with thy mouth the Lord Jesus, and shalt believe in thine heart that God hath raised him from the dead, thou shalt be saved.*" I do that now. I confess that Jesus is Lord, and I believe in my heart that God raised Him from the dead.

I am now reborn! I am a Christian—a child of Almighty God! I am saved! You also said in Your Word, "*If ye then, being evil, know how to give good gifts unto your children*: HOW MUCH MORE *shall your heavenly Father give the Holy Spirit to them that ask him?*" (Luke 11:13). I'm also asking You to fill me with the Holy Spirit. Holy Spirit, rise up within me as I praise God. I fully expect to speak with other tongues as You give me utterance (Acts 2:4).

Begin to praise God for filling you with the Holy Spirit. Speak those words and syllables you receive—not in your own language, but the language given to you by the Holy Spirit. You have to use your own voice. God will not force you to speak. Worship and praise Him in your heavenly language—in other tongues.

Continue with the blessing God has given you and pray in tongues each day.

You are a born-again, Spirit-filled believer. You'll never be the same!

Find a good Word of God preaching church, and become a part of a church family who will love and care for you as you love and care for them.

We need to be hooked up to each other. It increases our strength in God. It's God's plan for us.

About the Authors

Kenneth and Gloria Copeland the are best-selling authors of more than 60 books such as the popular *Walk With God*, *Managing God's Mutual Funds* and *God's Will for You*. Together they have co-authored numerous other books including *Pursuit of His Presence* and *Family Promises*. As founders of Kenneth Copeland Ministries in Fort Worth, Texas, Kenneth and Gloria are in their 31st year of circling the globe with the uncompromised Word of God, preaching and teaching a lifestyle of victory for every Christian.

Their daily and Sunday *Believer's Voice of Victory* television broadcasts now air on more than 500 stations around the world, and their *Believer's Voice of Victory* and *Shout!* magazines are distributed to more than 1 million adults and children worldwide. Their international prison ministry reaches an average of 60,000 new inmates every year and receives more than 17,000 pieces of correspondence each month. Their teaching materials can also be found on the World Wide Web. With offices and staff in the United States, Canada, England, Australia, South Africa and the Ukraine, Kenneth and Gloria's teaching materials—books, magazines and videos have been translated into at least 22 languages to reach the world with the love of God.

Learn more about Kenneth Copeland Ministries
by visiting our website at:
www.kcm.org

Books Available from Kenneth Copeland Ministries

by Kenneth Copeland

* A Ceremony of Marriage
  A Matter of Choice
  Covenant of Blood
  Faith and Patience—The Power Twins
* Freedom From Fear
  Giving and Receiving
  Honor—Walking in Honesty, Truth and Integrity
  How to Conquer Strife
  How to Discipline Your Flesh
  How to Receive Communion
  Living at the End of Time—A Time of
    Supernatural Increase
  Love Never Fails
  Managing God's Mutual Funds
* Now Are We in Christ Jesus
* Our Covenant With God
* Prayer—Your Foundation for Success
* Prosperity: The Choice Is Yours
  Rumors of War
* Sensitivity of Heart
* Six Steps to Excellence in Ministry
  Sorrow Not! Winning Over Grief and Sorrow
* The Decision Is Yours
* The Force of Faith
* The Force of Righteousness
  The Image of God in You
  The Laws of Prosperity
* The Mercy of God
  The Miraculous Realm of God's Love
  The Outpouring of the Spirit—The Result of Prayer
* The Power of the Tongue
  The Power to Be Forever Free
  The Troublemaker
* The Winning Attitude
  Turn Your Hurts Into Harvests

* Welcome to the Family
* You Are Healed!
  Your Right-Standing With God

by Gloria Copeland
* And Jesus Healed Them All
  Are You Ready?
  Build Your Financial Foundation
  Build Yourself an Ark
  Fight On!
  God's Prescription for Divine Health
  God's Success Formula
  God's Will for You
  God's Will for Your Healing
  God's Will Is Prosperity
* God's Will Is the Holy Spirit
* Harvest of Health
  Hidden Treasures
  Living Contact
  Living in Heaven's Blessings Now
* Love—The Secret to Your Success
  No Deposit—No Return
  Pleasing the Father
  Pressing In—It's Worth It All
  Shine On!
  The Power to Live a New Life
  The Unbeatable Spirit of Faith
  This Same Jesus
* Walk in the Spirit
  Walk With God
  Well Worth the Wait

Books Co-Authored by Kenneth and Gloria Copeland
  Family Promises
  Healing Promises
  Prosperity Promises

  From Faith to Faith—A Daily Guide to Victory
  From Faith to Faith—A Perpetual Calendar

One Word From God Series
- One Word From God Can Change Your Destiny
- One Word From God Can Change Your Family
- One Word From God Can Change Your Finances
- One Word From God Can Change Your Health

Over the Edge—A Youth Devotional
Over the Edge Xtreme Planner for Students—Designed
    for the School Year

Pursuit of His Presence—A Daily Devotional
Pursuit of His Presence—A Perpetual Calendar

Other Books Published by KCP

The First 30 Years—A Journey of Faith
    The story of the lives of Kenneth and Gloria Copeland
Real People. Real Needs. Real Victories.
    A book of testimonies to encourage your faith.

John G. Lake—His Life, His Sermons, His Boldness of Faith
The Holiest of All, by Andrew Murray
The New Testament in Modern Speech,
    by Richard Francis Weymouth

Products Designed for Today's Children and Youth

Baby Praise Board Book
Noah's Ark Coloring Book
Shout! Super-Activity Book

Commander Kellie and the Superkids Adventure Novels

- #1 The Mysterious Presence
- #2 The Quest for the Second Half
- #3 Escape From Jungle Island
- #4 In Pursuit of the Enemy

SWORD Adventure Book

*Available in Spanish

We're Here For You

Join Kenneth and Gloria Copeland, and the *Believer's Voice of Victory* broadcasts, Monday through Friday and on Sunday each week and learn how faith in God's Word can take your life from ordinary to extraordinary. This is some of the best teaching you'll ever hear, designed to get you where you want to be—*on top*!

You can catch the *Believer's Voice of Victory* broadcast on your local, cable or satellite channels.

*Check your local listings for more times and stations in your area.

Believer's Voice of Victory

Enjoy inspired teaching and encouragement from Kenneth and Gloria Copeland each month in the *Believer's Voice of Victory* magazine. Also included are real-life testimonies of God's miraculous power and divine intervention into the lives of people just like you!

It's more than just a magazine—it's a ministry

S H O U T !
...the faith-filled magazine just for kids!

Shout! The Voice of Victory for Kids is a Bible-charged, action-packed, bimonthly magazine available FREE to kids everywhere! Featuring *Wichita Slim* and *Commander Kellie and the Superkids. Shout!* is filled with colorful adventure comics, challenging games and puzzles, exciting short stories, solve-it-yourself mysteries and much more!

Stand up, sign up and get ready to Shout!

To receive a FREE subscription to *Believer's Voice of Victory*, or give to a child you know a FREE subscription to *Shout!*, write:

Kenneth Copeland Ministries
Fort Worth, Texas 76192-0001
or call:
1-800-359-0075
(9 a.m.-5 p.m. CT)

World Offices
of
Kenneth Copeland Ministries

For more information and a free catalog,
please write the office nearest you.

Kenneth Copeland Ministries
Fort Worth, Texas 76192-0001

Kenneth Copeland
Locked Bag 2600
Mansfield Delivery Centre
QUEENSLAND 4122
AUSTRALIA

Kenneth Copeland
Post Office Box 15
BATH
BA1 1GD
ENGLAND

Kenneth Copeland
Private Bag X 909
FONTAINEBLEAU 2032
REPUBLIC OF SOUTH AFRICA

Kenneth Copeland
Post Office Box 378
SURREY, BC V3T 5B6
CANADA

UKRAINE
L'VIV 290000
Post Office Box 84
Kenneth Copeland
L'VIV 290000
UKRAINE

Learn more about Kenneth Copeland Ministries
by visiting our website at:

www.kcm.org

The Harrison House Vision

Proclaiming the truth and the power
Of the Gospel of Jesus Christ
With excellence;

Challenging Christians to
Live victoriously,
Grow spiritually,
Know God intimately.